Keep the Changes!

52 Tools for Successful Living

&

Solutions You Can Take Home

Jef Herring

Keep the Changes!

52 Tools for Successful Living
&
Solutions You Can Take Home

ISBN: 0-7392-0076-3
Library of Congress Catalog Card Number: 99-94034

Printed in the USA by

MORRIS PUBLISHING

3212 East Highway 30 • Kearney, NE 68847 • 1-800-650-7888

Publisher: Success & Change Technologies and Strengthening the Family Press
1589 Metropolitan Blvd. Suite A
Tallahassee, FL 32308

CONTENTS

Success-Stress-Motivation-Change

Families - Teens - Parenting

Marriage - Couples - Relationships

Acknowledgments

all the many people I want to thank......

Now I know what people mean when they say "there are so many people to thank and I hope I don't miss any......"

My thanks and appreciation go out to so many people, not necessarily in this order:

- the hundreds of individuals, couples and families over the years, who have patiently taught me what works and what doesn't. I hope you have learned and grown from our time together as much, and even more, than I have.

- the readers, friends and colleagues who stop me in public, write letters, make calls, send emails, etc. who have encouraged me and told me how much you enjoy the column. There is no way for you to know how many times you have made my day!

- and to my lovely wife Lauren, who encourages me, helps me juggle all my blessings, and most of all, loves me and encourages me every day to "walk my talk."

My heart felt thanks and sincere appreciation goes out to all of you.

Keep the change!

Jef

Introduction

and suggestions about reading this book.......

Welcome to my first book of columns, "Keep the Changes!: 52 Tools for Successful Living & Solutions You Can Take Home." Keep the Changes! is comprised of 52 columns from my weekly column on relationships, life, success and change. I've set it up so that you can read one column a week for a year. At the end of each column, you'll find a series of "action questions" designed to help put some "hands and feet" on the tools and solutions you have just read.

Of course, you can read more that one column a week. It's just set up so that if you implement the tools and suggestions in each column once a week for a year, I'll bet you will notice a difference in your life.

One of my biggest frustrations with the typical self help/motivational/inspirational book is that it's relatively long on description and short on solutions. For example, let's say you walk into the bookstore and purchase a book on self esteem. If it's 100 pages long, here's what you are likely to find: 99 pages describing the problem, defining the problem, giving you the history and examples of the problem, and perhaps even telling you how the problem is experienced in other countries. Which leaves about 1 page for "oh by the way, here's what you can do about it, if that's why you really bought the book."

Drives me nuts!

So, what I have focused on in this book is the same thing I do in speaking, writing, or in personal consultation/coaching sessions. And that's to provide you with at least 4 key benefits:

☞ *solutions you can take home*
☞ *tools for successful living*
☞ *put "hands & feet" on change*
☞ *knowing exactly what to do next.*

And to that end, it's time to say enough introduction! Let's move on into "solutions you can take home & tools for successful living."

Thanks for reading, and as always.........

Keep the change!

Jef Herring
November 1998

Success

Stress

Motivation

Change

"Everything should be made as simple as possible, but no simpler."

Albert Einstein

Solutions Start With The Right Questions

"A very well-asked question can almost answer itself."
Jef Herring

A good counselor knows how to ask good questions. Many times people will come in to my office asking "Why do I feel this way?", and then tell their story.

After hearing their story, I change their question into "How could you not be feeling this way?"

With a simple question, we can normalize their feelings and begin to put things in a different perspective for change.

A well asked question provides at least two immediate benefits: 1) it gives a person direction, in terms of what to do next, to get the changes they desire, and 2) when a question is asked very well, it can often provide the answer itself.

One of my recent favorites that falls into this category is the following question, "What's currently in your life that you would like not to be there and what is currently not in your life that you would like to be there?" A powerful question. Let's take a closer look at each part of this question and then some tips for how to answer them in your own life.

"What's currently in my life that I would like not to be there?" This question focuses on getting rid of or eliminating something from our life. What might it be for you? Is it a habit that you no longer like, such as smoking, eating too much, losing your temper, or something else? Could it be a behavior pattern, such as working too hard, choosing relationships that are destructive, being too nice and letting people take advantage of you? Or is it a fear, or even a phobia, you would like to eliminate, perhaps a fear of flying, of people, of success? Whatever it is for you, there are four key steps that you can take when you have decided to remove something from your life.

- 1) Reach the level of ENOUGH

Reaching the level of "I have had ENOUGH" is a very powerful motivator for change. As humans we are very adaptable and can put up with quite a bit when we must. Reaching the level of enough can sometimes be like filling a glass with water one drop at a time. The glass will hold a great volume of water, and then one more little drop sends the water cascading over the side, resulting in sometimes massive change. At the same time, we have to be careful about how much we will tolerate before changing. Scientists (how did they think of this one?) have found that if you throw a frog into a pot of boiling water the frog will do everything it can to get out to avoid being cooked. On the other hand, if you start the frog out in a pan of lukewarm water and slowly increase the temperature to a boil, the frog will stay in the pan and get cooked alive.

The good news is, you don't have to wait until you're about to be "cooked alive" to have reached the level of enough. If you can stand just one more metaphor, being ready for change can be like taking an elevator going down - you can decide what floor to get off on.

- 2) Decide/commit to the change

The root word for decision means "to cut off." Commit means to leave no other option open. So deciding and committing simply means to allow for no other option than for the change. Failure then is no longer an option. This involves moving from "I want to want to" to I will change no matter what.

- 3) Focus your energy.

Take all the action steps necessary to allow the change to occur. If you are wanting to stop smoking, and you leave cigarettes in your desk drawer, you are not focusing your energy or taking action steps for change. Focusing your energy means doing *all the necessary things* to remove something from your life.

• 4) Replace the negative with something positive.

It can be very difficult to remove something negative from your life without replacing it with something positive. One hint is to ask yourself this question "when this is no longer in my life, what would I like to have there instead?"

Which leads to the second part of the question, "what is currently not in your life that you would like to be there?" Would you like a better job, more money, less stress, more fun, better relationships, or something else? Whatever it is for you, there are three steps you can take to add what you would like to your life. I call them the "3 D's of change."

• DECIDE that something has to be different.

Similar to reaching the level of enough, deciding that something has to be different means you have committed to adding something positive to your life. Now is the time, and there is no room for excuses. Which leads to the need to......

• DO everything necessary to get the changes you want.

This means taking all the necessary action steps to get what you want & doing it on a giant scale. Read about it, go to seminars, find out all you can. Because success leaves a trail, find someone who has done what you want to do & find out how they did it. No need to reinvent the wheel. While you are taking giant action steps toward what you want, learn to.........

• DISTINGUISH between the actions that are working and the actions that are not.

Watch yourself and the world around you to see if you are getting the results you want. Keep the actions and beliefs that are working and discard and change the ones that do not work.

3

Wow, look at all the strategies for change we got out of just one well asked question. As you begin to make changes in your life, remember the power of well asked questions. And one more thing, remember to enjoy the journey.

ACTION QUESTIONS

1) What questions do you ask your self that get in the way?
2) How will you now change the quality of your questions?

Making Changes

"Too many of us get stuck in 'I want to want to"
Jef Herring

Do you remember the old story about the guy that comes in to the doctor and the doctor asks him what's wrong? The man says, moving his wrist back and forth, "It hurts when I do this." And the doctor says, "Well, don't do that!"

Wouldn't it be nice if all changes were that easy? Many people have a great deal of difficulty with changing what they want to change. In helping people to get the changes they want, I have found at least two major myths that are hindrances to change. One myth is the belief that change will take a very long time. This is fostered, in part, by some of the popular notions about therapy perpetuated by the media. You know the drill, you come in to the shrink week after week for years, lay down on the couch, and talk about yourself while someone nods their head and says, "Uh-huh", over and over.

While it's true that some problems can take awhile to solve, many problems can be solved and real change achieved in a relatively short period of time. Additionally, while I do have a couch in my office, I'm the only one that ever lies on it, when I take a nap during a long day.

Another myth is that the therapist will somehow make you change, that there is some magic to the process. While I have seen some fairly "magical" changes in people, it's my belief that when a person is ready to change, they will find a way. We just help them in the process.

It's like the old joke, "How many therapists does it take to change a light bulb?" "Just one, but the light bulb has got to really want to change."

5

When it comes to a person's desire and readiness to change, there are basically three categories. They are:

- "I want to want to"
- "I want to"
- "I'm going to/ I will."

• <u>Stage one: "I want to want to"</u>

The "I want to want to" stage is characterized by an acknowledgement that a change needs to take place, there is simply little or no motivation to do so. Often there are shoulds or oughts involved. "I really ought to lose weight", or "I really should stop smoking." Another characteristic of this stage is that the motivation for change lies in another person, such as a spouse or parent who is pressuring the person to change. The likelihood of any significant change is remote.

• <u>Stage two: "I want to"</u>

The "I want to" stage is also characterized by an acknowledgement of a need for change, with some minimal motivation as well. Many people at this stage will use the two most fatal words when it comes to changing, the words "I'll try." What's wrong with saying "I'll try?", you may be asking. The brain doesn't understand I'll try. Here's what I mean. Try and pick up the newspaper or book you are reading right now. Did you pick it up? Then you picked it up, you didn't "try", you simply did it. You either do it or you don't. That's all our brain understands. Our brain interprets I'll try as just noise and no change takes place.

• <u>Stage three: I'm going to/ I will"</u>

This stage is marked by an acknowledgement of the need to change, a great deal of motivation to do so, and the *decision* to make the change. The root word for decision is the same as for the word incision, which means to cut. So the word decision means to cut off any other possibility but the desired change.

6

If you find yourself in one of the first two categories, how do you get yourself motivated to make the decision for change? Anthony Robbins, the well known motivational speaker, offers us some assistance here. Robbins uses a technique called the "rocking chair" technique to help motivate you for change. For whatever change you are deciding to go for, fast forward your life to the time you will be old and sitting in your rocking chair looking back on your life. Then ask yourself two questions:

- How does it feel looking back, not having made the changes you wanted?
- How does it feel looking back, having made the changes you wanted?

These questions can greatly increase your ability to decide and your motivation for change.

The process of change can be difficult enough without being bogged down in the first two stages. Getting to stage three, where you have decided "I will change this" gives you the motivation necessary for change.

Thanks for reading, and keep the change!

ACTION QUESTIONS

1) Do you really want to change, or do you just want to want to or want to?

2) What decisions could you make, right now, that would move you into "I will change?"

Clear and Simple Change

If you don't know where you are going,
any road will get you there.

Helping people to make the changes they want in themselves and in their relationships is a very rewarding way to make a living. I remember in graduate school how we studied several different theories of counseling. Every counseling theory had it's own theory of change, each one more complicated than the last.

One of the main things I wanted to do out in the real world was to find the simplest and most profound methods for helping people get the changes they desire. In the process I've gotten some criticism for trying to make change too simple. Maybe so, but I guess I agree with Albert Einstein's' quote, "Everything should be made as simple as possible, but no simpler." I think change can happen in the same way. I suppose I could make change more complicated, but why??

One of the best methods I have found for simple and profound change is being very, very clear about the outcome you want to happen. The clearer your outcome is the easier it can be to reach. This is called having a "well-formed outcome." I owe this idea to Ed and Maryanne Reese of the Southern Institute of Neuro Linguistic Programming in Florida. There are six basic steps to getting a well-formed outcome. Each step involves asking just a few key questions:

Step 1

- State your goal in the positive. A useful question would be "What do I want?" This is a crucial step because the brain cannot picture negatives. Try this little experiment for example. Try to picture a woman not riding a bike. Easy you say, I'll picture a woman running. But that's not a woman not riding a bike, it's a woman running. In the same

8

way, if your goal is to stop yelling at your spouse, then you will need to state what you will be doing instead, such as communicating in a more loving fashion. Some people may say that this is *just* semantics. My answer is that it is *all* semantics. The language we use for change is crucial.

Step 2

- <u>State your goal in terms that can be seen.</u> In other words, if I had a video tape of you before, and a video tape of you after you reached your goal, what differences would I notice? What would a camera pick up that is different? Using our example, you could say you would be spending more loving conflict free time with your spouse.

Step 3

- <u>State the goal in a way that is under your control.</u> A good question would be "What do you need to get it?" While you can control how you speak to your spouse, you can't control whether they clean the sink or not. Make sure you have a goal where no one else needs to change except you.

Step 4

- <u>Check to see if it fits into your world.</u> An obvious question is "What do you stand to gain from this change? "A not so obvious question is "What do you stand to lose?" Are you willing to give that up? An example would be someone who wants to stop getting sick or hurt so often and be a healthy person. They may have to give up all the attention involved in being hurt or sick.

Step 5

- <u>Be specific about your goal.</u> When do you want it? When do you not want it? While it's usually a good thing to not yell at your spouse, you might want to be able to yell if they are about to be struck by a car. A silly example, but you get the point.

Step 6
- <u>State your goal in a way that is testable.</u> In other words, can you demonstrate that you have met your goal? How do you know things are different? One of the key questions I ask my clients is, "How will you know when we have been successful with your changes?"

The almost magical feature of this process is that when it is done carefully and in detail, the problem can be virtually solved. Or at least the next step and direction can be crystal clear.

ACTION QUESTIONS

1) Choose a goal (outcome) you want in your life and go through all six steps above.
2) Make sure your outcome is crystal clear.

Riding the Waves of Change

"The goal is to become a master of change"
Jef Herring

When I was a kid I had a surfboard. To call myself a surfer would be a gross over exaggeration. I just sort of played at it at best. These thoughts occurred to me recently during a few days at the beach, trying to slow down the end of summer.

While playing in the surf it also struck me that playing in the waves is a great metaphor for dealing with change. Much like change, a wave is a force you just can't fight. There are really only three choices when it comes to dealing with a wave. You can let it knock you down, you can find a way to survive it, or you can ride it and make it work for you.

Much like the waves coming in to shore, change is powerful and inevitable. It can also be incredibly stressful. No one really likes change, except perhaps a baby with a wet diaper. It's up to us to decide how we are going to handle change and the stress that comes with it. As motivational speaker and trainer Brian Tracy says, "we can either be masters of change or victims of change."

Here are three ways to handle the waves of change -
♦ Getting Knocked Down

You just can't successfully fight a wave. It will knock you down. In the face of change, many people will says things like, "This just isn't fair", "This shouldn't be happening", or the dead end question, "Why does this always happen to me?"

All these are symptoms of what is called the "dead roach approach" to change. If you have ever seen a dead or dying roach, you know what I mean. They just sort of roll over on their backs and kick their feet in the air. They assume a very powerless position, and just allow whatever happens to happen.

11

The dead roach approach is a sure fire prescription for becoming a victim of change.

♦ Surviving

Another way to approach a wave is to hold on for dear life and let it take you where it may, hoping to just survive. And that's the main question in merely trying to survive the waves of change - "How do I survive this?"

While at first glance this may seem like a reasonable approach, it really isn't. Asking the question of "how do I survive this?" teaches us to merely get by, to do the minimum necessary to make it.

In the long run, it's simply a well disguised prescription for becoming a victim of change.

♦ Riding and Thriving

My experience with helping people deal with the changes is their lives has taught me that there is a better way, an optimal way, to deal with the changes in our lives. It involves moving from the mind set of mere survival, to a notion I call "thrival."

The concept of thrival involves two key ingredients:
• making the very best of what comes your way
• making it work for you.

It involves asking a very powerful question when faced with change. This small but profound question is simply, "In how many ways can I make this work for me?" This simple question allows our brain to tap into our natural creativity and find ways to thrive in any situation.

Here's an example of how to thrive in any situation. Hockey great Wayne Gretsky was asked in an interview what he thought it was that made him so successful. He humbly stated that there were many players who were better and more gifted as athletes. He explained his phenomenal success in this way, "Most guys go to where the puck is. All I do is *go to where the puck is going.*"

It's been said that one of the best ways to predict the future is to create it yourself. Asking the question of how can I make this work for me empowers us to create the circumstances that will allow us to successfully ride the waves of change. This is a prescription for becoming a master of change.

The choice is yours. You can be a "dead roach", a survivor, or a master of change. Which will it be for you?

ACTION QUESTIONS

1) Think of a time you took the "dead roach approach."
2) Think of a time you merely survived.
3) Think of a time when you really thrived.
4) Which did you like better?

The Many Myths of Change

"Change takes a long time and is very hard"

When I was a kid of about 8 or 9 years old, my parents gave me a dollar to go to the store with a friend and his parents. At the store, I found a Frankenstein model that I wanted for 88 cents (I realize I'm dating myself with that price). I told my friend's mom I wasn't going to get it because it was 88 cents, I had a dollar and I didn't want to lose the 12 cents difference. My friends mom then explained to me that the clerk would give me the 12 cents back when I bought the model. So I bought it.

What's the point? *No one had ever explained the concept of change to me.*

In my work with helping people get the changes they want, I have found the same to be true for many people. *No one has ever explained the concept of change to them.*

For instance, who made the rule that change has to be hard or take a long time? These are two of the many myths about change that hold people back.

Let's explore a few of the myths about change and some of the quick, simple and powerful ways to bring about the changes we want in our lives.

- Myth 1 - Change is hard.

There are certainly times when change can be difficult. Notice I said difficult and not hard. The distinction between hard and difficult is much more than semantics. When something is difficult to change, it only means that it takes commitment and constant attention to change. Unfortunately, we sometimes seem more committed to the belief that something is hard than we are to changing it. How many times do you think you have to say something is hard before it becomes easy?

- Myth 2 - Change takes a long time.

Sometimes the process of change can take a while, but the decision to change can be done in an instant. Recently, an acquaintance mentioned they were considering going back to school to become a doctor. "But," they said, "I'll be 8 years older when I graduate." I then asked, "How much older will you be 8 years from now if you don't go back to school?"

The bottom line is this - we change when we decide to change. And not a second sooner.

- Myth 3 - I can't change unless and until (someone else changes first, I get a better job, it's warmer outside, etc. etc. etc.).

The reality is that when it comes to getting the changes we want, we either get them or we have reasons why we didn't. It's amazing to me how incredibly intelligent, motivated and creative we are when it comes to finding reasons why we couldn't change. If we simply used our intelligence and creativity to make the changes we want, it would simplify and speed up the whole process.

- Myth 4 - Change is complicated.

Not really. Change is in fact very simple. We are complicated. When you break it down to bare bones, change really involves only three steps. I call them "the 3 D's of change" -

* 1) Decide something has to change
* 2) Do all the necessary things to achieve the change
* 3) Distinguish between what is working and what is not. If it's working, keep doing it. If it's not, go back to step two until you find what works.

Almost all failure to change can be traced back to a violation of one of these three steps. We get in the way and complicate the process. To quote a wise and learned person, it was Pogo who said, "We have met the enemy, and he is us."

Now let's take the general guidelines above and make them more specific for each of you. Think back to a time in your life when you decided to change something, did all the necessary things to change it, and got the changes you wanted. Now ask yourself three key questions -

- What were the specific things I thought and believed to get the change?
- What were the specific things I did to get the change?
- What were the specific things I believed and did to keep the change?

The answers to the above questions give you your specific strategy and pattern for change. Simply apply them in the present to get the changes you currently desire.

In closing, remember that change can be easy. It's we who are complicated. Thanks for reading. *And keep the change.*

ACTION QUESTIONS

1) What were some of the myths about change in the family in which you grew up?
2) What is a myth about change that you have now?
3) If you haven't already done so, go back and answer the questions in this column.

The Gift of Problems

*"There is a time in the life of every problem
when it is big enough to notice
and small enough to solve."*

I recently came across the above quote and love what it has to tell us about solving problems. For most of us, problems are one of the greatest sources of stress in our lives. Whether problems come in the form of relationships, self-esteem, financial, career, or some other form, they can bring a great deal of stress into our lives.

It's my belief that while problems do bring stress and are important to properly handle, our response to the problem is more important than the problem itself. How stressful a problem is can be determined to a large extent by our response to it.

Many of us have learned avoidance as a way of handling problems. "If I just ignore this, maybe it will go away" is what we think. If you hear an alarming noise in your car, just turn up the radio. No noise, no problem!

Richard Bach, author of Jonathan Livingston Seagull and Illusions, has this to say about problems, "there is no such thing as a problem without a gift in it's hands. We seek problems because we need their gifts." What would it be like, instead of avoiding problems, we were to "lean into them" and seek their gifts?

In order to lean into problems, we have to approach them in a different way. A major source of stress from problems comes from doing the same things over and over again and expecting different results. If we are to successfully handle problems, we need to be able to look at them in a different way. As Albert Einstein said, "You cannot solve a problem with the same level of thinking that created the problem." We

17

need creative problem solving skills that allow us to not only learn from the problem, but have fun and strengthen us as well. Here are three creative ways to approach the problems in our lives.

- "Movie Solutions"

Often the difficulty is that we have only our view of the problem with which to work. So what would it be like to get a variety of different perspectives on the solution to the problem? Here's a simple three step process for getting a different perspective-

1- Hold a problem in your imagination for a moment.

2- Think of a favorite actor/actress or a movie you have seen that you strongly related to.

3- Ask the question, "how would this person have approached and solved this problem?"

You may get solutions from this exercise or only a different way to look at the problem. Either way is a win. Use your own judgement about the appropriateness of the solutions.

- "Question Solutions"

Motivational expert Tony Robbins offers us five questions for approaching problem solving in a different way. They serve to help us reframe our approach to the problem. The five questions are -

1- What's good or great about this situation?

2- What's not perfect yet?

3- What am I willing to do to solve this problem?

4- What am I willing to no longer do to solve this problem?

5- What actions can I take that will help me solve the problem *and* enjoy the process?

- "Crazy Solutions"

Lastly, let's look at a process that I typically use to help parents solve power struggles with their teenagers. It's applicable for our purposes as well. Here are the six easy steps.

18

1- Identify the problem.

2- Identify one or two solutions that you have tried that just don't seem to work, and then discard them.

3- Come up with crazy, ridiculous, absurd, outlandish solutions *that you would never do,* but are absolutely fun to think about. The purpose here is to get you laughing at and about the problem in order to get a better perspective.

4- Come up with creative alternative solutions to the problem. Sometimes the seeds for these creative ideas are in the crazy ideas. Other times you have simply been able to step back far enough from the problem to be creative.

5- Once you have your creative solutions take massive action toward solving the problem.

6- Pay attention to the results you are getting. If it's working, you can keep doing it if necessary. If it's not working, repeat steps 3 - 5 until you get a solution that works.

What we have looked at is three simple approaches to creative problem solving. Have fun trying them out in your own life. My guess is the opportunity will present itself soon, maybe even today.

If you have other solutions that work for you, I would love to hear about them. We'll put the best suggestions into a future column. Thanks for reading, and keep the change.

ACTION QUESTIONS

1) Which "movie solutions" can you use to change your life right now?

2) Which "question solutions" can you use to change your life right now?

3) Which "crazy solutions" can you use to change your life right now?

The Power of Optimism

"The optimist says the glass is half full; the pessimist says the glass is half empty. I say the glass is too darn small"
George Carlin

There are many important questions to answer in life. Questions such as "who am I", "where will I go to school", "what do I believe in", "what will I do for a career", "who will I marry"; and the list goes on and on.

One of the most important questions that I believe effects all the others is the old worn out question "is the glass half empty or half full? The answer to that question controls your outlook on life, whether you are a pessimist or an optimist.

The interesting thing is that it really doesn't cost you anything to be an optimist. So you may get disappointed more often than the pessimist, but you also get to experience more of the passion of life.

Here's what I mean. Harnessing the power of optimism allows you to do at least three key things vital to success in life. The power of optimism allows you to think the right thoughts, ask the right questions and dream the right dreams to enable you to live to your full potential.

Let's take a closer look at each of these three key factors.

• The Right Thoughts

This concept has nothing to do with mind control or any other Orwellian idea. What is does have to do with is the ability to control your own thoughts. Because if you can control your thoughts, you take a major step toward controlling your life.

OK, class, let's have a quick little lesson on the ABC's of emotions. This is simply a three step process for successfully handling our thoughts and emotions. First, we have a fact or an event (A). Then we have our beliefs or thoughts about the fact or event (B). Our feelings are the result of our thoughts and beliefs (C). The result of this ABC process is the actions we then take.

It follows that if we think and feel in a positive way, we will then take positive actions in our life.

• The Right Questions

Closely related to the first ingredient, asking the right questions helps us to focus our energy like a laser beam. In many ways our brain is simply a very advanced computer. The old saying "garbage in, garbage out" means that if you ask garbage questions you'll get garbage answers. If you ask powerful questions you'll get powerful answers.

Here's an example. All of us have too much to do. Under the stress of too much to do we often ask "How will I ever get all this done?" That's a garbage question that leads to garbage answers like "I don't know" or "I'll never get this done." A more useful and empowering question might be, "How can I get all this *and more* done, *and* have a good time doing it?" Do you see the difference?

Now I know some folks out there are saying "Oh c'mon, isn't this just semantics?" My answer to that is when you consider the power of language for change, it's *all* semantics.

• The Right Dreams

One of the things I have learned in my work with people is that each one of us has dreams for our life. In the words of singer Billy Joel "everybody has a dream." What's yours? Are you living it? Have you given up on it? In how many ways could you find your way back to your dream?

I've noticed another interesting thing while working with people on their dreams. Most of us dream too small. It's almost as if we are afraid to dream too big. My suggestion is it's a whole lot better to fall just short of a big dream than it is to fall short of a small dream.

Here's a couple of questions specifically designed to help you in discovering or rediscovering your dreams:
- "If you could design your life any way you wanted it, how would it be?"
- "What will your life look like when you are living out your dreams?"

Thinking the right thoughts, asking the right questions and dreaming the right dreams allows us to harness the power of optimism in our lives. See how each of these key ingredients can empower your life in the coming days, weeks and years.

ACTION QUESTIONS

1) How might you need to change your current thoughts, questions and dreams into ones that are more supportive of who you want to be?

"That's Just Where It Starts, With a Dream"

"Everybody has a dream"

Billy Joel

When I was in high school in the seventies, I met a woman in our church who every one called "Ma" Parker. Ma Parker was the kind of person that kids in a church will flock to - she provided a listening ear, unconditional love, and lots of good food. She also seemed to have a hotline to God and a piercing pair of eyes that caused you to tell the truth when she would ask "So tell me, how are you doing, son?"

I remember sitting in her kitchen one day as a junior and talking about what I thought I might like to do with my life. When I was in high school in the '70's, The Bob Newhart Show was popular. You know, the one they now show on Nick at Nite where Bob Newhart plays the therapist and every one walks around saying "HI, BOB." Now for some reason, I had always been the person that my friends talked to about their problems. It had occurred to me one day, listening to a friend and having seen Bob Newhart the night before, that maybe I could actually make a living doing something I seemed to enjoy. I was telling Ma Parker all about this idea one day and then ended my excitement by saying "But that's just a dream.' She turned to me and with that piercing stare said the following words that have greatly influenced my life - "That's just where it starts, with a dream."

So let's consider for today the power of dreams. Not the movies you see in your head while sleeping, but the kind of dreams about what you want to do and be in your life.

As we grow up all of us have dreams about what we would like to do with our lives. In the words of Billy Joel,

23

"everybody has a dream." The happiest people among us seem to be the ones that are living out their dreams in some way as adults. Still others don't seem to be living out those dreams. If you find yourself in the category of not fulfilling your dreams, I wonder what happened? Some people lose sight of their dreams, others may see their dreams die, still others have forgotten what their dreams once were. Some are still struggling to see their dreams come true.

Whatever the reasons for not living out your dreams, working with people has taught me to be enough of an optimist to believe we can still dream again. So, if you were to dream again, what would it be about? How is it similar to and different from earlier dreams you had for your life?

Now that I've hopefully got you dreaming just a bit, let's consider some ways to turn dreams into reality. While it's all well and good to dream, for them to become real we have to take action toward the dream. I think Richard Bach, in his book "Illusions" (Dell Books, $4.95) says it well, "You are never given a wish without the power to make it come true. You may have to work for it however."

In my experience the working at it involves setting goals for yourself. Setting goals to work toward your dreams is simply breaking your large dream down into manageable pieces. A wise person once said, "A goal is simply a dream with a deadline."

Now if you are at all like me, I sometimes get a little tired of all the talk about goal setting. Sometimes my attitude is "Yeah, yeah, I've heard this before, goals are important." But check out this piece of information. A study was done on a group of Harvard graduates involving the power of goals. This group was tracked for a number of years and some interesting and powerful things were discovered about the power of goals. Of this group of graduates, only 3% had goals that were written down. The amazing thing was that at the end of the study, the 3% that had written goals were worth more in financial terms than the other 97% combined. Keep that notion in mind as you work on your goals.

Having said all that, here are some questions and ideas to get you started -

• Are you living out any of your dreams?

• If yes, good for you - and consider what it took and what you did to get there.

If no, what got in the way? Is it possible to resurrect any of the old dreams?

• If you were to dream again, what would it be about?

Once you've begun dreaming again, here are some things to consider -

• What have I learned from dreams that did not work out that I can use now?

• Break your dream down into manageable goals for the year, month, week and even day.

• What are you doing on a daily, weekly, monthly basis to work toward your goals?

Dreams and goals, when properly directed, can allow us to enjoy a very full life. Get started today on your own goals and dreams.

And by the way, thanks a bunch Ma Parker!

ACTION QUESTIONS

1) What dreams are you living?
2) What dreams have you let slip?
3) What would it take to resurrect them?
4) What would it be like to create some new dreams?

Breaking the Rules Can Be Good for You

"Rules are made to be broken"

The average teenager

Rules. The Rules. It seems like we have heard a great deal about this topic lately. Several books and talk shows seem to be focusing on all the different rules for life. We have *The Rules* by Ellen Fein and Sherrie Schneider, *The Southern Rules* by Ellen Patrick, and so on and so on.

At the same time, have you ever stopped to consider what the rules are for your life? I'm not talking about things like make your bed, brush your teeth and be at work by 8am. Instead, I'm referring to the sometimes faulty emotional rules that govern the way we think, feel, and live.

Of all the sources of stress in our lives, faulty emotional rules are one of the most debilitating. These faulty emotional rules are typically ingrained during childhood and become an unquestioned part of how we live our lives. Because they are largely unquestioned, we rarely stop and consider how they might be influencing our lives. If unchecked, they can even *rule* over us.

"How can I know what these rules are if they are out of my awareness?" Good question! Perhaps a few examples will help to illustrate what I mean.

The first example involves a person who appeared to have their life all together. They were fulfilling most of the dreams and were financially secure. Yet they always felt like there was something missing.

If this scenario sounds familiar, you're not alone. It's a fairly big club.

Now, check out what we discovered about this person's faulty emotional rules for life. The rules were:
1) I have to be perfect.
2) If I'm not, then I make a fool of myself.
3) Then I'll never forgive myself.
Not exactly a prescription for enjoying life, is it?

Let's look at another example, if you will. This person was in and out of bad relationships, and had a pattern of being taken advantage of by others. Here are the rules this person lived by:
1) I have to please everyone around me.
2) If I don't, then I am bad.
3) Then people will leave me.

Are you beginning to see the pattern here? Faulty emotional rules typically involve three steps or parts that look something like this:

- 1) I have to.............. This usually involves some kind of command, with no choice involved.
- 2) If I don't, then I'm.......... Usually something bad and difficult to change.
- 3) Then (fill in the blank) will happen. Some terrible event that will dramatically effect the rest of your life, maybe even threaten your life.

Now that we have established the pattern of how these rules are developed, what are some of your faulty emotional rules for living that get in the way? Simply ask yourself these three questions:

- 1) In order to be a good person, what do I believe I have to do?
- 2) If I don't, then what does that make me?
- 3) Then what will happen to me?

The answers to these questions can give the basics of the faulty emotional rules you may have been living by, without even knowing it.

"Alright, now that I've identified some of these rules, how do I go about changing them?" Another good question.

Here's one of the rare places in life where you are not only encouraged to break the rules, you'll be breaking them for a good purpose. One way to begin to break and then change faulty emotional rules is to ask lots of challenging questions about them. For instance -

- where did they come from?
- who taught them to you?
- in what "emotional classroom" did you learn them?
- are they useful rules?
- do you want to keep them, change them or get rid of them?
- are they outdated and no longer applicable?
- are they like training wheels on a bike - necessary for survival at one time but no longer needed?

These questions can begin to loosen the hold that these faulty emotional rules have over you.

The next step is to begin to construct and create your own emotional rules that fit in your present life. One way to do this is to ask around among friends and family about what rules seem to work for them. They might look at you strange at first, but if you keep digging, you may find some interesting things.

Another way is to find someone you admire and either guess about their rules and/or ask them.

Still another way is to ask yourself "what do I need to believe in order to feel the way I want to feel, take the actions I want to take," etc.

All of us either have, or have had, faulty emotional rules in our lives. The trick is to identify, challenge, break, and then most importantly, change them. Thanks for reading, and keep the change.

28

ACTION QUESTIONS

1) If you haven't already done so, go back and answer the questions in this column.

2) What one faulty emotional rule, if you committed to changing it, would dramatically change the quality of your life in the next year?

When was the Last Time You Had Fun?

"All I wanna do, is have some fun."
Sheryl Crow

"All I wanna do, is have some fun. I got the feelin', I'm not the only one." These lyrics won singer Sheryl Crow the honors of Record of the Year and New Artist of the Year at the 1995 Grammy Awards. I've got the feeling that her lyrics have tapped into a longing of most us.

All I want to do is have some fun. Interesting lyric. In our complicated, fast paced, over worked and over scheduled society, when was the last time you had some fun?

According to Stephen Glenn, author of Raising Self-Reliant Children in a Self-Indulgent World, the average American family spends only 14 1/2 minutes a day together. Twelve of those minutes are spent disciplining, correcting and planning how to get through the next day. Which leaves about two and a half minutes for all the other things families are supposed to do. The January/February issue of the Family Therapy Networker, a publication of the American Association for Marriage and Family Therapy, is entitled "Breathless - Spinning through our time-starved lives." In the Networker, the following disturbing statistic and quote is found, "The average working couple in America spends only *20 minutes a day* sharing time together. Is it surprising that this couple has difficulty communicating? Or that they feel less and less intimate as the years go on. Or that one half of these marriages end in divorce? When you consider the demands on their time, it's obvious that a major source of disorientation and anger experienced within families is quite literally a matter of how they must spend their time..........."

Many of the families and couples I work with seem to feel exhausted all the time by the demands of an average week. Get up, get ready for work, get the kids ready for school, go to work, come home, eat dinner, get the homework done, get the kids to bed, (or if they are teenagers, make sure they are home), collapse in front of the TV, go to bed. Get up and do it all again. Rinse and repeat.

Then the weekend comes and along with it the illusion that we'll get some rest and get some things done. The frenetic pace of the week seems to intrude into the weekend as well. All the things we've bought as convenient time savers simply serve to increase our stress level. Again, according to The Networker, "Time-saving devices don't really save time; they merely shorten tasks. What we experience is a frustrated sense of continual interruption." Sound familiar?

While I was writing this article, I came across an issue of Newsweek entitled "Exhausted." In an article entitled "Breaking Point", Newsweek reports that "The Annals of Internal Medicine recently reported that 24 percent of people surveyed complained of fatigue that lasts longer than two weeks (*my guess is in reality the percentage is much higher*). Fatigue is now among the top five reasons people call the doctor. People are frayed by the inescapable pressure of technology, frazzled by the lack of time for themselves, their families, their PTAs and their church groups. They feel caged by their jobs, even as they put in more overtime. We are fast becoming a nation of the quick, or of the dead tired."

Our fast paced lifestyle is not just a phenomenon of the 90's, however. In the film Broadcast News (1987), Holly Hunter plays a character who is so over scheduled and stressed out, she has to schedule time to cry. In the movie, each night she sits on the edge of her bed at a certain time and cries for five minutes. Then she moves on with her schedule.

31

Where did this all come from? I was in graduate school when I reluctantly bought my first appointment book. Now it's not unusual to see some of the adolescents I work with carrying their own schedule planner.

If you want to learn more about how we got to this place, read the Newsweek article. I guess I'm not as interested in how we got here as I am interested in what to do to cope with it.

Here's an exercise that can provide a quick check up on your stress level, when was the last time you had some fun, and then what to do about it..

Take a sheet of paper and list all the activities you can think of that you do for fun. These can be things you've done recently, a long time ago, or just things you would like to do and haven't yet. Be sure to include both small things like reading a book, and larger things like taking a vacation. After you have created your list, look it over in the following manner: next to what you have done today, put a D, this week, a W, this month, an M. For things you've only done in the last three months, put a 3, in the last six months, a 6, and only in the last year, a 1. For things you have never done put a N. Leave everything else blank.

Now look over your list. What does it tell you about the amount of fun in your life? If you are like most of us, you are light on D's, W's and M's, and heavy on 3's, 6's, and 1's.

So what to do? You don't have to quit your job or fly off to Tahiti to balance things out. Although it might be nice. A simpler approach would be to just pick one item from your fun list and commit to doing that activity in the coming week. Pick one more the next week, another the next week, and so on. In this way, you get 100% improvement each week.

How's that for progress?

ACTION QUESTIONS

1) What stops you from having the fun you want to have in life?

2) If you haven't already done so, DO NOT read further until you complete the fun exercise above.

Self Esteem and Pizza

"Self-esteem is like a pizza"

Jef Herring

Self esteem. Now there's a well used and little understood term. Self esteem seems to be one of those terms that we frequently use without really knowing exactly what it means. Just what is this self esteem thing? And where do you go to get some? I've never seen a self esteem store at the mall. Not yet any way.

Many people tend to define self esteem as the way you feel about yourself, which seems to be a little redundant. For the sake of this column, let's define self esteem as the perceptions and beliefs you have about yourself.

Having said all that, let's focus in on a quick and simple way to improve your self esteem.

One of the quickest and simplest methods for improving your self esteem is simply to rate it on what I call the Self Esteem Rating Scale (SERS). Here's how it works: on a scale of one to ten, with one being the worst and ten being the best, rate your self esteem in these four ways-

1) what it is now
2) the worst it's ever been
3) the best it's ever been
4) how you would like it to be

Now, having done that (if you haven't done that, go back and do it before you read on, it just takes a few seconds!) consider these things:

- What were you doing when it was the worst that you might need to eliminate?
- What were you doing when it was the best that you might need to resume doing, continue doing, or do more of in the future?

- If your self esteem now is higher than the worst it's ever been, what did you do to change it that you might want to continue to do ?

Now take a look at the difference between what your self esteem is now and what you would like it to be. The difference is the ground you need to cover to improve your self esteem. Now for a seemingly bizarre and unrelated question. How do you like your pizza? Just bare with me here. However you like it, what would happen if you tried to eat an extra large version of it in one bite? That's right, you couldn't do it and would probably choke. So you slice it into smaller pieces and then take even smaller bites to accomplish the task.

It's the same way with self esteem. For example, let's say your self esteem is now a five and you would like it to be a ten. That's a difference of five self esteem levels. If you tried to jump from a five to a ten all at once, you would probably become frustrated, discouraged and give up. It's just too big a leap.

What you can do is begin to break it into manageable pieces by asking yourself "What will it take to move from a five to a six, a six to a seven?" , and so on. In this way you are biting off manageable chunks that will give you the opportunity to achieve small successes, which can then motivate you on to the bigger successes of accomplishing your self esteem goal.

While using the Self Esteem Rating Scale can be a quick and easy way to improve your self esteem, that's not to say it won't involve some struggles. And that's a good thing because I believe there is value in the struggle. A patient of mine recently shared the following wonderful story about butterflies and the value of struggling.

Now if you have ever had the privilege of watching the amazing process of a butterfly leaving its cocoon, you know its quite a struggle. Well, it seems some scientists, in their esteemed wisdom, found a way to get butterflies out of their cocoons without a struggle. What they found however, was that the butterflies that had to struggle out of their cocoons lived longer, flew better, and were more beautiful than the butterflies that were removed without a struggle.

Besides saying something about the value of the struggle, I believe it also says something to us about the difference between science and success!

Maybe it's like something Tom Hanks said in the movie "A League of Their Own." One of the players was complaining about how hard something was and Hanks responded, "Of course it's hard. That's what makes it good." Or perhaps it's like I say to many of my clients who want to change their self esteem, "I won't promise you the struggle will be easy, just worth it."

ACTION QUESTIONS

1) What's your current level of self esteem?
2) What would it take to raise it just one level?
3) What are you waiting for?

The Incredible Power of Choice

"In the beginning was the word,
and the word was choice."

Tom Robbins

"In the beginning was the word, and the word was choice."
I often use this quote to begin workshops on motivation and
self esteem. The quote comes from a poem in a novel by Tom
Robbins, which I'll share more of later in this column.

For now, have you ever considered the incredible power of
choice in our lives? Now, choice is a concept that has become
strongly linked to the issue of abortion. While an important
issue, this column has nothing to do with the abortion issue.

What this column does have to do with is how the power of
choice in our lives is essential to living a full and vital life. In
fact, I would go so far as to say that our ability to make
choices is a large part of what makes us human. If you can
grasp the power of our ability to choose, it can literally change
your life. And yet so many of us are either unaware of, or
worse, deny the power of choice in our lives.

It's always amazing to me how skilled we are at denying
our ability to choose. I realize that I'll be dating myself with
this example, but do you remember the comedian Flip Wilson
and his character that always said "the devil made me do it?"
This is a great example of how we deny our ability to choose
and therefore deny responsibility as well.

The power of choice can be a frightening thing because, by
definition, it makes us responsible for our lives and our
choices. Consider this notion if you will: what we are today is
simply the sum total of the choices we have made so far in our
lives. But what about all the bad things that have happened to
me, you say? Often times we do not choose many things that
happen to us. What we can almost always choose is how we

respond to them. The things that happen to us can either beat us or better us. Even in the worst situations, we still have the power to choose our reactions and especially our attitude.

OK, I'm convinced, choice is important. So how do I practice the power of choice? Here are some small ideas to get you started.

- Pay attention to your language. Each time you catch yourself thinking or saying "I have to" or I should", see it as a signal to stop and consider the options you may have. Do you have to or do you want to or are you simply choosing to? What other choices do you have?
- Take responsibility for the choices you make. If you have made some bad choices that have got you where you are now, simply choose to accept things as they are and commit to begin making better and healthier choices in your life.
- Watch out for the trap of either/or choices. So many times we limit ourselves to only two choices, hence the "either/or trap". Many times there are a whole range of choices and alternatives if we only take the time to look.
- Simply practice choosing. Exercise your choice muscle by practicing making choices in your daily life.
- So many times we don't make choices simply because "that's the way I've always done it before." Remember, the only difference between a rut and a grave are the dimensions.

So now that you have some beginning ideas to get you started, allow me to close with the poem I mentioned earlier. It's amazing the places where you can find wisdom. I found this poem about fifteen years ago in a novel by Tom Robbins titled "Still Life with Woodpecker" (Bantam Books, $5.99). Here's the poem in part -

The word that allows yes,
The word that makes no possible.

The word that puts the free in freedom
and takes the obligation out of love
The word that throws the window open
after the final door is closed
The word upon which all adventure,
all exhilaration, all meaning, all honor depends
The word that the cocoon whispers to the caterpillar
The word that separates that which is dead
from that which is living.
In the beginning was the word
and the word was
CHOICE.

ACTION QUESTIONS

1) Practice each one of the above tips for a week.
2) How can you apply the poem to change your life?

"Sunday Night Syndrome"

*"We tend to go from Saturday Night Live
to Sunday Night Dread"*

Jef Herring

Picture, if you will, the following scene - It's almost Sunday evening, the weekend is winding down, and you're beginning to think about the work week ahead. What are your feelings? Do you find yourself excited and challenged, looking forward to another week of doing something you love? The most fortunate among us get to feel that way on a regular basis.

Or are you feeling something else? Perhaps some nervousness or anxiety, even a sense of dread? Did you know that what you are feeling has a name? It's a special kind of anxiety and stress that I call "Sunday Night Syndrome." What's Sunday Night Syndrome? It's when you think of the coming work week and experience anything from mild anxiety to severe dread.

All of us experience some form of Sunday Night Syndrome (hereafter called SNS), from time to time. The important thing is how often and how severe is it for you. Let's take a closer look at the different levels of SNS and then what to do about each.

Mild SNS

As I mentioned above, all of us experience a mild case of SNS from time to time. Symptoms can typically include a minimal level of nervousness and anxiety.

The anxiety usually begins on Sunday evening as you are preparing for the next day. These feelings seem to pass quickly and are gone by Monday morning when you arrive at work. One way to think of them is as a product of continually working five days a week and only having two off in which to recover.

- What to Do -
- relax - and remember the feelings will pass.
- rent a movie, play a game, enjoy being with family and friends.

Moderate SNS

The next stage of SNS is characterized by increasing levels of anxiety as the work week approaches. The anxiety begins earlier in the day and doesn't seem to pass as easily as in the first stage. A key symptom of moderate SNS is kind of silly but makes sense at an emotional level - we begin to stay up later and later on Sunday night, in the hope that we can keep Monday morning from arriving. As a result, we feel sluggish and not rested on Monday morning, which leaves us ill equipped to deal with our feelings and the week ahead.

Other symptoms include increased irritability and inattentiveness around family and friends, as well as the beginning of decreasing work performance. Colleagues and supervisors may begin to notice changes at this point.

- What to Do
- In addition to the above suggestions, make sure you get to bed early enough to be rested for the next day. I realize I might sound like your mother here, but it works.
- Identify things in your job that you can feel good about, even look forward to.
- As crazy as it sounds, some clients have found that going into the office, or doing a little work at home, seems to help at this point.
- If going into the office is not possible, getting as prepared as possible can also help.

41

Severe SNS

The third level of SNS doesn't wait until Sunday to arrive. It begins on Saturday or even Friday after work. You've heard of "Saturday Night Live?" Well, this is Sunday Night Dread.

By the time Sunday evening rolls around, folks are experiencing severe anxiety and a strong sense of dread. Some people become physically ill at the thought of beginning another work week. Depression is common at this point, as well as drinking to try and calm the emotions.

- What to Do
- An important question to pay attention to at this point is "what are your emotions and body trying to tell you?" If you don't pay attention, the feelings will usually get stronger.
- It could be time to consider a change - either in the details of your job or perhaps an entire change of job or career.
- Consult a career counselor to look at what options you may have.
- Make sure you are doing something, from talking about it to physical exercise, in order to relieve the stress.
- You might want to seek counseling to help you manage the stress, emotions and decisions involved.
- Remember that if it's hurting you, it's likely not helping anyone else.

In addition to all of the above suggestions, there are three books that I have recommended before that you might find useful at this point.

- "Chicken Soup for the Soul at Work" by Jack Canfield and Mark Victor Hansen (Health Communications, $12.95)
- "Heart at Work" by Jack Canfield and Jacqueline Miller (McGraw-Hill, $14.95)
- "Care Packages for the Workplace" by Barbara Glanz (McGraw-Hill, $14.95)

All of us experience a form of Sunday Night Syndrome from time to time. If you recognize yourself in any of these categories, be sure to use the suggestions listed to help you through the process

ACTION QUESTIONS

1) Do you think you have a form of SNS?

2) If so, which one?

3) What steps will you take to begin to deal with it?

Sharks & Dolphins at Work

*"Sharks and dolphins can look the
same in the water"*

Work. Of all the four letter words available to us in the English language, work can be one of the most distasteful. You may be reading this over your morning coffee, getting ready to start the work week. If you are one of the most fortunate among us, you get to do something for a living that you truly enjoy. You have a career. Or you may be in the group that does something for a living just to put bread on the table. You have a job. Whether you have a job or a career, the vast majority of us spend the majority of our waking hours working.

Handling the many stresses of work can be an exhausting experience. One of the most difficult stressors of work can be dealing with professional relationships. Whether you are dealing with a boss, a co-worker, or an employee, relationships at work can be a tremendous source of stress.

Let's take a look at two different ways of handling stressful relationships in the workplace. One of the most useful distinctions to make about work relationships is the difference between dolphins and sharks. Let me explain through the use of a metaphor. When you go to the beach, it's usually fairly safe to swim in the water with dolphins. Swimming with sharks, on the other hand, is a very dangerous activity. The trouble is, sometimes when you're in the water is can be very difficult to tell the difference between the dolphins and the sharks.

In the workplace, dolphins are the people you can trust. Sharks are the people that, at best, you can't trust, and at worst, you have to protect yourself against.

Let's take a look at some dolphin traits and some shark traits. See if you recognize anyone you work with or know.

- Dolphin traits
- do what they say they will do
- can be confided in
- team players
- their behavior matches their words
- take responsibility for mistakes
- can be trusted
- Shark traits
- fail to follow through
- can't be confided in
- out for themselves
- behavior doesn't match words
- blames others
- can't be trusted

The most dangerous kind of shark is the kind that behaves like a dolphin. If you will allow me to mix my animal metaphors, I think I can explain what I mean. There is the story of the beaver that was getting ready to cross the river. Just as he was getting ready to cross, he came upon a scorpion who wanted a ride across the river. The beaver refused, saying the scorpion would sting him and he would die. The scorpion denied this and promised he would not harm the beaver, if only he would take him across the river. The beaver, being a good natured and trusting chap, allowed the scorpion to crawl on his back and he swam across the river. Just as the beaver reached the shoreline, the scorpion stung him and got off. As the beaver lay dying, he asked the scorpion why he broke his promise. The scorpion replied, "I'm a scorpion, that's what I do".

And so it can be with some work relationships.

One useful way to handle the sharks and scorpions in your work life is to play the game called "I can expect that...." For most dolphin-like people, it usually comes as a surprise when people behave like sharks. It catches us off guard. It's difficult not to react in ways that are not helpful to us. Playing "I can expect that" simply means that with certain people we can expect them, almost trust them, to behave in shark-like ways. Playing "I can expect that" allows us to:

- anticipate negative behavior
- plan for negative behavior
- respond instead of react
- predict other's behavior
- reduce our stress level

After a little practice, you can even laugh a little at what's happening - "here it comes, I was expecting that". Here's an example of the benefits of playing I can expect that. A client I once worked with, (let's call her Mary) had a colleague who exhibited some distinctly shark-like behavior. Whenever Mary was in a staff meeting presenting an idea, her boss would shoot it down if she had no part in the idea. This was a particularly difficult behavior to confront because it could be easily denied by her boss. By playing the "I can expect that" game, Mary was able to arrive at a creative solution to the problem. Whenever Mary had an idea that she really wanted to see happen, she simply anticipated her boss's response, and ran the idea past her boss at least a week before the meeting. By doing this, she found that many more of her ideas came to fruition.

Now, some may call this being manipulative. I call it simply working smarter instead of harder. Mary anticipated her boss's behavior, created a plan to deal with it, responded instead of reacted, and significantly reduced her stress level.

We all have to deal with work relationships. Sometimes that means dealing with some difficult people. In order to reduce your stress level, identify the sharks, and when appropriate, try playing the "I can expect that" game. Good luck!

ACTION QUESTIONS

1) Who are some of the dolphins where you work?
2) Who are some of the sharks where you work?
3) Which one are you?

6 Strategies for Managing Stress

*"Most of us are all stressed out
and nowhere to go"*

She came in completely stressed out. Stress from all the areas of life was pressing in on her every day. Between her job, her children, her husband, and a few crises too close together, not to mention the rest of her life, she had reached the limit of her ability to deal with stress. In her own words, she was close to "losing it."

In the high stress world in which we live, it's all too easy to reach the point of feeling stressed out beyond our ability to cope. And yet it's our ability to cope that makes all the difference. I say this because stress is not going away. It's here to stay.

If ever you find yourself reading a book or in a seminar that says you can totally eliminate all your stress, either throw the book away or get out of the seminar! I'm sure these are nice people and mean well. They're just wrong! The reason for that rather strong statement is that it's not the elimination of stress, but the successful handling of stress that we need.

So let's look at six different strategies for successfully handling the stress in our lives. Each one can be used separately or in conjunction with the others.

- *Talk it out* - Whatever we don't talk out, we act out. That's sort of a basic rule of mental health. If we don't talk about it, it's sure to come out in some other way.
- *Take mini-vacations* - One of the misconceptions about handling stress is that we can push hard all year (or maybe longer) and then expect that all the stress can be healed in a one or two week vacation. It just doesn't happen. Our bodies, minds, and spirits need more frequents breaks than once a year. This is especially true if you are one of those

people that schedules a vacation like a typical work day, so you can get the most out of it. The result is you return home needing a vacation from your vacation.

- *Distinguish between stress and pressure* - Stress comes from the outside. Pressure, on the other hand, is an inside job. Pressure is what we tell ourselves about the stress. My belief is that we can handle almost any amount of stress if we are handling our thoughts about it in a positive way. I read a quote recently that said, "All the water in the ocean can't sink a ship unless it gets inside." Sometimes, something as simple as "I can handle it" is all we need to keep the stress outside of us.
- *Create your own relaxation triggers* - This is an exercise I teach in every stress seminar I do. It involves three simple steps that allow you to relax anywhere, any time.

Step 1 - Picture yourself in a very relaxing place. Create as much detail as you can in the picture, making it bright and colorful. (If you are reading this in traffic, I strongly suggest not to do this exercise. Put the paper down and drive.) Make sure you are seeing the scene through your own eyes, as if you were there. See it, hear it, and feel it.

Step 2 - While you are picturing yourself in this place, create an immediate trigger that will instantly remind you of the relaxed feeling. It could be a snap of the fingers, a word or phrase, or a mental picture. Anything that quickly and strongly reminds you of your relaxing place.

Step 3 - When you find yourself in a stressful situation, simply go for your relaxation trigger, fire it off, and feel the almost instant relaxation.

- Here's an interesting one - *stop worrying!* I know that sounds too simple, but just consider it for a moment. What good, what change has come about from worrying? So why do it? "But I don't know what else to do", you say? Read on.

- *Take action* - taking action, doing something about your stress or your worry is an instant sure fire cure for worry. It's very difficult to worry if you are busy doing something about it.

We began this list with the suggestion of talking about your stress. It's a good thing to do, most of the time. It can become a bad thing, though, if that 's all you do. To be successful in making stress work for you, you simply have to take action. Here's where I think Nike got it right with "just do it."

I realize that taking action or "just do it" may sound too simple. I suppose I could make it more complicated for you, but why?

So there we have it, six strategies for making stress work for you. Here's one more suggestion - practice one of these a day for the next six days. At the end of six days, you'll have a strong and rich tool bag for dealing with stress. And remember - "All the water in the ocean can't sink a ship if it doesn't get inside."

ACTION QUESTIONS

1) What distinctions do you need to make between stress and pressure?

2) How could the quote "no amount of water can sink a ship if it doesn't get inside" improve your life right now?

Too Many Hats

"One day I'm a mother,
One day I'm a lover,
What am I supposed to do?"
"Workin' for a livin'
All because I'm driven....
Why do I have to wear
So many things on my head?"
Amy Grant

These lyrics in the Amy Grant song "Hats" seem to capture the cry of many over worked, over whelmed and stressed out people. In the song , the word hats simply refers to all the different roles we must play in our every day lives. All of us wear many different "hats" in our day to day lives. There is the hat of employee, parent, spouse, son or daughter, etc., etc. It might be easier if all of these hats could be worn one a time, we could complete one role and move on to the other. Unfortunately for most of us, we tend to wear all of our different hats in the same day, often at the same time.

The responsibility and pressure of too many hats at once seems to be a unique kind of stress all its own. I call it Too Many Hats Syndrome (TMH). TMH Syndrome can be likened to the side show at the circus where the guy has several plates spinning on sticks all at once . He has to constantly run around to make sure he keeps all the plates spinning.

Let's take a look at some of the signs of Too Many Hats Syndrome, and then some ways to cope with this particular brand of stress.

Signs of THM Syndrome

- always doing something, rushing rushing rushing
- never enough time
- not able to have fun and/or relax

51

- trouble falling asleep
- waking up during the night and not being able to go back to sleep
- a feeling of always "being on"
- isolation thinking - "I'm the only one who has this much to do"
- the sense that if you stop and rest, everything will fall apart
- working in bed, right up until the time you try to sleep
- feeling exhausted all the time
- fantasies of running away from it all

Coping with TMH Syndrome

One of the most misleading ideas about coping with stress is the faulty notion that somehow we can eliminate stress from our lives. If you are alive, you are experiencing some level of stress. In fact, it's a sign that you are alive. The main solution is in how we respond to and therefore cope with stress. Dr. James Loehr, in his book "Toughness Training for Life" (Penguin Books, $11.95) has this to say about dealing with stress; "Stress management systems usually aim at reducing stress, an unrealistic goal for most of us." Instead, Loehr focuses on how to be".....emotionally strong enough to thrive on the stress" in our lives.

Unless we win the lottery or become independently wealthy in some other way, most of us will simply have to learn how to cope with our own version of "Too Many Hats." Here are some suggestions for thriving on stress, instead of just surviving:

- Organize, organize, organize your time. If you are saying you don't have enough time to organize, you're proving my point.
- Pay attention to how you talk to yourself about your stress, your self-talk. Negative self talk such as "How will I ever get all this done?" or "This is just not fair!" turns

stress into pressure. Positive self talk allows us thrive on the stress in our lives.

- Learn to say no when your dance card is already full. Keep handy a 3x5 card with the word NO written in big black letters
- Reframe the stress from "all I have to do" to "all I get to, or all I am able to do".
- Delegate - another sign of TMH syndrome is the mistaken belief that we are the only ones who can do a task properly. If it can be done by someone else, allow them the privilege of helping.
- Reminding yourself of how you usually do get everything done can calm you and put things in perspective
- To get a different perspective on the situation, consider how a favorite character from a recent movie or TV show would handle the situation
- Mini-vacations - whether a three day getaway or a five minute break, getting away refreshes us. In order to thrive through our stress, we need periods of recovery time.
- Remember this word - BALANCE - make sure to leave room for the hat called fun and relaxation.

Stress is an inevitable part of our daily lives. To be able to thrive on our stress, it's important to have fun and to enjoy keeping all those plates spinning.

ACTION QUESTIONS

1) Are you wearing too many hats?
2) Which ones could you take off?
3) And what's stopping you?

The Power of Belief

"I believe I can fly"
R Kelly

Of all the talks and presentations I am privileged to give, perhaps my favorite is one called "The BRAAVO Approach to Life." In this talk, we look at six key factors involved in building your self-esteem, setting and reaching goals, and basically leading a life well lived. The acronym BRAAVO stands for Belief, Responsibility, Asking, Action, Vision and Opportunity.

Today's column begins a series of columns looking at each of these six key factors. In this column we will look closely at the power of belief. Consider, if you will, these five quotes about the power of belief:

◆ "As a man thinketh, so is he" - Proverbs
◆ "Whether you believe you can or you believe you can't, you are right" - Henry Ford
◆ "Argue for your limitations and you get to keep them" - Richard Bach
◆ "I believe I can fly. I believe I can touch the sky." - R Kelly
◆ "If it's possible in the world, it's possible for me." - Author Unknown

There we are, from the Bible to pop music, the power of belief comes through in a big way. The power and strength of belief in our lives cannot be overemphasized. It is the first key building block in self esteem and success. Like a house built on solid ground, self esteem and success built on belief will not be washed away by the storms of life.

Self-esteem Is Belief In Yourself

As I have studied the concept of self esteem over the years, I have found scores of definitions. As I have asked people in my office, groups and seminars for their definition, most people have said something like "Self esteem is how you feel about yourself." That's very close, but there's just one problem. Feelings can easily change. In my experience, belief is stronger than feelings because often times belief can be an act of the will.

So the working definition of self esteem that I have found most useful is simply THE AMOUNT AND STRENGTH OF BELIEF IN YOURSELF.

"Given that definition, how can I raise my self esteem and belief in myself?", you may be asking. Good question.

Let's go back to the quotes about belief from the start of this column. For each quote, we'll look at a series of questions that will begin to give you some solutions you can take home.

"As a man thinketh, so is he"

- What consistent thought patterns do you have that get in the way of belief in yourself?
- What thoughts can you begin to focus on that would increase the strength of your belief in yourself?

"Whether you believe you can or you believe you can't, you're right"

All of us have been told that we could not do or accomplish something. Then we believed what we were told. Therefore we didn't even try.

So allow me to ask you these questions-

- What if they were wrong? What could change in your life?
- What is something you have always believed you could not do?
- What could happen if you changed your belief?

A wise person once said, "Successful people are too busy accomplishing things to pay attention to the people that say it can't be done." What do you need to get busy doing?

"Argue for your limitations and you get to keep them"

- What are some of the limitations you have argued for in the past?
- What are some of the limitations you still argue for?
- Isn't it time to stop? What could happen if you did?

"I believe I can fly. I believe I can touch the sky"

This quote goes from a focus on just getting by or survival, to a state I like to call "thrival."

- What would it look to "fly" in your life?
- What would it look like to "touch the sky" in your life?
- What would "thrival" look like to you?

"If it's possible in the world, it's possible for me."

This is my personal favorite. The world is full of examples of people accomplishing incredible things. We still live in a world full of opportunity. Just look around you.

- If anything were possible, and you knew you couldn't fail, what would you do?
- As you look around your world, who has or is accomplishing something you would like to do? Remember that if they can do it, so can you.

Well, I've certainly asked you a bunch of questions, haven't I? The point of all these questions is simply this - a well asked question sets up the conditions for change and allows to find solutions you can use in your own life. My challenge to you is to use these questions, and more importantly, the answers, to increase the power of belief in your life.

ACTION QUESTIONS

1) Answer and apply each of these quotes about the power and strength of belief.
2) One suggestion would be to focus on one a day for an entire week.

Avoiding the Ruts and Holes of Life

"The first rule of ruts - when you find yourself in one, stop digging."

Sounds so obvious doesn't it?

And yet we keep falling into the same holes and ruts just the same. We know something doesn't work and yet we keep doing the same things over and over again.

Have you ever wondered why we do this? And more importantly, how do we stop doing it, how do we stop "digging"? And how do we get out?

As I've studied and searched over the years for ways to help people get the changes they want, quickly, gently and effectively, I've stumbled across a poem that seems to capture well the process of change.

It's called "An Autobiography in Five Short Chapters." Let's look at each of these chapters, and what they have to teach us about the process of change.

♦ *Chapter One - "I walk down the road. There's a big a hole in the road. I don't see it. I fall in. It's not my fault. It's dark and scary. It takes me a long time to get out."*

We've all had the experience of winding up in a hole and wondering how we got there. It seems like we were minding our own business, and all of a sudden we wind up in a situation we never intended. Or as Jimmy Buffet once sang, "......trying to figure out how I ever got here."

♦ *Chapter Two - "I walk down the road. There's a big a hole in the road. I don't see it. I fall in. It's not my fault. It's dark and scary. It takes me less time to get out."*

Here we go again. If the first time came as a surprise, this is getting to be a habit, or a pattern.

Denial and blame tend to show up at this point in the game. Denial says "what do you mean, what's my part?" Blame says "someone else did this to me, and just wait until I find them!"

At this point we are still digging the hole, and are just not aware of it yet. This is where the rut begins. It's important to remember that "the only difference between a rut and a grave are the dimensions."

♦ *Chapter Three - "I walk down the road. There's a big a hole in the road. I see it.* I fall in anyway. *Maybe I've got something to do with this. It's dark and scary. I get out."*

Don'tcha just hate it when you know better, you even know you know better, and yet you wind up in the same place again?

Here's when change can begin to occur, because we begin to see our part in the problem. Good questions to ask are -

• What's my part in this?

• What am I willing to do to change this?

• What am I willing to stop doing to change this?

It's also important to remember my favorite definition of stuck is "when we keep doing the same things over and over again and expect different results."

♦ *Chapter four - "I walk down the road. There's a big a hole in the road. I see it. I walk around it."*

Good job! You're starting to pay attention, and make progress. Here's the not so good news. It's not enough. "What do you mean, it's not enough? Didn't I stay away from the hole?" Yes, you did. And while that's good, in the words of southern rock group Molly Hatchet, your "flirtin' with disaster."

"Why is that?" Because you are still on the same road, and human nature has a curious feature. We tend to forget how bad things were, and we can fall into the trap of checking out the hole "just one more time", just to make sure it was really that bad. Like an alcoholic in a bar or a dieter at an all you can eat buffet, you are flirting with disaster.

♦ *Chapter Five - "I walk down a different road."*

While chapters one through four do involve some amount of change, it's still not real change. There's lots of movement and things may even look different, but it's still "change without change."

The real change, that is transformation, can go something like this four step process -

- you do the same thing again and then realize it afterwards
- you do the same thing again and realize it while you are doing it
- you realize you are about to do the same thing before you do it, and do something different
- you automatically do something different

The beauty of "walking down a different road" is that transformation has taken place. Not only do you no longer fall in the old holes, you find that you don't even want to. They no longer hold any interest or attraction for you.

It's a goal worth attaining.

ACTION QUESTIONS

1) What chapter are you in, in your life?
2) What chapter will you be in this time next year?
3) What do you need to do to make it happen?

Families

Teens

Parenting

"Trying to control a teenager is like trying to put pants on a gorilla. It's just going to frustrate you and make the gorilla really mad"

Jef Herring

Universal Laws for Raising Teenagers

"Exactly when did we lose control?"

Exasperated parent

Q: *"We have two children, ages 10 and 12, who are about to enter the teenage years. We have had relatively little trouble so far and would like to keep it that way, as much as possible. Are there any general guidelines for parents of teenagers?*

A: These are wise parents! They are asking for guidelines and assistance *before* any problems arise, and thus are thinking preventatively. There's a proverb that says "raise up a child in the way they should go and when they are old they will not depart from it." What that implies is that at some point they will move away from it. These parents are preparing for that time.

Not only can I offer them some guidelines, I'll go so far as to offer them some "universal laws" on the raising of teenagers. A universal law in the physical world is something like gravity. It doesn't matter if you ignore it, don't believe in it, or don't think it applies to you. If you violate the law of gravity by jumping off a high building and haven't arranged for a gentle glide or a soft landing, you will go splat. In the same way, violate any of these universal laws for raising teenagers once too often, and you might go splat as a family.

♦ The Law of Belonging

The greatest need of teenagers (after music and the phone) is a strong sense of belonging. They need to feel like they are a part of something bigger than themselves. If they don't get it in a healthy place (family, healthy friends, clubs, sports, youth groups, etc.) they will get it in an unhealthy place, such as negative friends, drugs, gangs, or cults. The parent's job is to make sure they get it in a healthy place, even if they don't like it all the time.

One way to do this is to require that a child, from the earliest age possible, belong to some kind of group. It can be school, recreation, or church related, as long as they experience a sense of belonging.

The time will come when they no longer want to be a part of a particular group. That's acceptable, as long as they replace it with some other type of healthy group belonging.

◆ The Law of Hope

Recent statistics show that the only group where the suicide rate continues to rise is that of adolescents.

It's my belief and experience that this results directly from a lack of hope. Hope for the future, hope that things will get better, hope that they can change.

One of the things I do with teens in my office is have them bring in their favorite music, along with lyrics. With some music, my challenge to them is this, "Find me one place in here where there is any hope, and I won't ever bring up your music again." Many times they can't.

So here's a question: "Do you know the lyrics of the music your kids are listening to?"

◆ Law of Power

Once you have entered into a power struggle with a teenager, you have already lost. It's like the closing line of the movie "War Games", "Interesting game, the only winning move is not to play".

Does that mean to let them do whatever they want? Of course not! Remember the old Dodge commercial, with the two rams butting heads on the mountain, with the slogan "Dodge Trucks are ram-tough?" That always looked to me as if it hurt.

It's the same way with power struggles, you might win the battle, but you hurt or lose the relationship.

♦ Law of Control

I've said this before, but it bares repeating. Trying to control a teenager is like trying to put pants on a gorilla. It's just going to frustrate you and really irritate the gorilla. Not a great way to live day to day.

♦ Law of Management

A management approach to raising teens puts the parents clearly in charge. The goal is to eventually manage them out of your lives, and into their own. Parenting is one of those jobs where the goal is to eliminate the need for your job.

♦ Law of Voice

In a well functioning family, the teens almost always get a voice. They just don't always get a vote. Consistently violate either side of this equation and you've got trouble.

♦ Law of Modeling

If you don't want your teen doing something, make sure you are not doing it yourself. Teens have very strong and sensitive "hypocrisy meters" and are very eager to use them.

♦ Law of Punishment

Punishment is often done out of anger and is usually for the parent. Punishment breeds resentment and a desire for revenge. Teens have many creative ways to get you back.

♦ Law of Consequences

Consequences teach teens about the real world. In general they need to be related, reasonable, respectful, swift, strong and short-term.

♦ Law of Structure, Part 1

Parents need to set boundaries and structure from day one. If you don't do it while they are young, what in the world makes you think they will obey curfew when they have a car?

◆ Law of Structure, Part 2

We over structure the time of children and under structure the time of teenagers. Teenagers need boundaries and structure just as much as children do, if not more.

◆ Law of 20 Feet

The law of 20 feet states that at a certain age, you must walk at least 20 feet away from your teen if you are in a public place. Thirty feet if you're in the mall.

◆ Law of W's

When teens are gone from home, parents need to know who they are with, where they are going, what they will be doing and what time they will be back.

I hope these laws help get you started on managing the teen years. I'm sure some of the veteran parents out there have some additional laws that they have found helpful. I'd love to hear from you and perhaps highlight them in a future column.

ACTION QUESTIONS

1) Which of these universal laws have you violated on a consistent basis?

The Top 10 Things Never to Believe from Your Teenager

"Mom, it's not my fault"
any teenager

While working with families with teenagers, there is never a dull moment. While helping families through this difficult stage, I sometimes get accused of being down on teenagers. Nothing could be further from the truth. In fact quite the opposite is true. One of the reasons I enjoy my work so much is that teenagers have so much energy, are so bright, and basically are just so alive. My wife tells me that one of the reasons I like working with them so much is because I'm still a teenager myself. While I tend to disagree, I sure have fun working with them.

Having said all that, let's take a look today at what I call "The Top Ten Things Never To Believe From Your Teenager*, *unless you have solid, irrefutable, total, you saw it proof."

- 1) <u>It's not my (pot, beer, cigarettes, etc.), I'm just keeping it for someone else.</u>

Yeah right. The next question for the parent to ask is, "If you are keeping this for your friend, what is your friend keeping for you?" One of the reasons parents can get fooled here is that you so desperately *want to believe* that it is not theirs and they are not doing drugs. It's important to remember that this is something your teen might be counting on.

- 2) <u>When caught with drugs - This is just the first time I've tried it.</u>

Unlikely. Usually when kids get caught with and/or using some drugs, they have been doing it awhile. They have simply slipped up, gotten caught, and are trying to find a quick way out of it.

- 3) We don' have homework in that class

Sometimes this is true. Or they have already done it at school. Often times it's a good excuse for not doing homework, or for covering up for skipping class. Either way, it's one of the easiest to check out by talking with the teacher. Which parents need to be doing anyway.

- 4) The teacher doesn't like me

Maybe so. This is usually just a handy excuse for bad grades or getting in trouble. Either way, it's the kid's job to find a way to make it work, even if the teacher doesn't like them. It's simply practice for the real world, where not everyone is going to like you; sometimes even bosses or co-workers.

The interesting thing about this one is the teen's solution to the problem. It goes something like this - "Well, the teacher doesn't like me, so I'll show them by flunking the class." And who is this hurting?

- 5) Of course there will be parents at the party

The answer to this one is, "If that's true, then you certainly won't mind me calling up your friend's parents to see if there is anything I can do to help."

6) Everyone else gets to do it, so why can't I?

Another popular one designed to make parents feel guilty and old fashioned, so they will give in to something they think is wrong. My mother had a wonderfully confusing answer to this one; "If everyone else stood on their head in the middle of the street at three in the morning in their underwear, would you?" Probably would have.

- 7) Everyone drinks and smokes. There's not a single person my age who doesn't.

Many, many teenagers do. But not each and every one. I know of plenty who do not and have a very good time with

65

what they do. Another one designed to get parents to tolerate behavior they don't like.

- 8) "If you let me off just this once, I'll promise I'll never do it again."

Another one parents want so badly to believe. Unfortunately, what the teenager usually learns here is that the parent really doesn't mean it about consequences. While in some ways it might be easier to let them off the hook, it teaches very little about the real world.

- 9 *and* 10) "Give me one good reason why I can't do that!"

This one gets two places because it is so common and so important. The crucial part not to believe here is that they are really asking for a legitimate answer to the question. After giving a well reasoned adult answer, here is something you will not hear from your teenager, "Well, thank you for explaining it that way to me folks! And now that you have, not only do I no longer want to do that, I'm embarrassed and ashamed for asking. Please forgive me and good night." If that ever happens, call me right away because something is very wrong!

So there you have it. The Top Ten Things Never To Believe From Your Teenager. This is just a sampling, there are many more of course. I'd like to invite parents to let me know some additional "not to believes" they have discovered.

In the meantime, keep a skeptical and loving ear attuned to what you hear from your teens.

ACTION QUESTIONS

1) Which of these do you recognize?
2) Which of these have you been fooled by?
3) If you really want to have a fun family discussion, take this list to your teenager and see how many they will admit to.

The Top 5 Things Never to Say to Your Teenager

*"When I was your age......*from any parental lecture

I recently wrote a column called "The Top Ten Things Never to Believe from Your Teenager." Some friends and colleagues wondered if I was giving away too many secrets or if the teenagers would be mad at me. The funny thing has been that most of the kids read the column on our bulletin board, and not only tell their parents which ones they do, they add more to the list. Go figure.

So here's a column to sort of balance things out on the parent's side. I offer The Top Five Things to Never Say to Your Teenager. All of these spring from positive, although misdirected attempts by parents to get some kind of change. Alternative suggestions are offered for each.

- 1) "You're grounded for life!"

You never want to say anything, even in anger, that you cannot back up or follow through on. When you do, it teaches your teen 1) that you don't mean what you say, and 2) to not take you seriously. There is also another problem with grounding anyway. In order to have a prisoner, there has to be a jailer, and I doubt that you would want to play that role for the rest of your child's life.

You might try this - ask your teen what they think a fair consequence might be. Oftentimes, they come up with something harsher than you ever would have.

- 2) "I'm thoroughly disgusted with you."

Or something similar. It's perfectly ok to be angry, frustrated, even disgusted by your child's behavior. What you don't want to do is to shame your teen. The crucial distinction to be made here is the difference feeling ashamed and feeling shame. While these two words are only separated by the letter "a", they are vastly different in emotional impact. Ashamed is the appropriate guilt we feel when we have *done something wrong*. It allows for change. Shame is what we feel when we believe we *are something wrong*. It doesn't allow for change. It's "I don't like what you did" vs. "I don't like who you are."

- 3) "Why can't you be more like (fill in the blank)."

The infamous comparisons. This one seems so innocent, and yet can be so disabling. The message sent is that you are not good enough as you are, and must measure up to some other standard in order to be loved. If you want a clear picture of the results that are possible from comparisons, check out the classic movie "Ordinary People."

An alternative would be to ask your teen what characteristics they might like in the person you are tempted to compare them to.

- 4) "When will you ever learn?"

From the same family as "why can't you ever.....", and "how many times have I told you", these are what Jane Nelson and Lynn Lott, authors of "Positive Discipline for Teenagers" call "adultisms." This has nothing to do with adultery. We commit an adultism when we forget what it's like to think, act and perceive the world as a child and then expect a child who has never been an adult to think, act and perceive the world like an adult. They won't unless we teach them.

An alternative would be to simply ask, "what were you trying to accomplish by (fill in the blank)."

- 5) "When I was your age....."

If you don't believe this one is useless, just watch your teen's eyes the next time you say this one. You will see them glaze over as they go into the "I've got to sit through this again" trance. They hear absolutely nothing you say after "when I was your age."

Step back a moment and consider what you are trying to teach them. In doing family therapy, I will often ask a parent, in front of the teen, "what were you like when you were 16?" The teen is usually listening intently and gets to see a side of the parent they may have never seen before.

An alternative is to work this information into everyday conversation, without the dreaded "when I was your age."

Here's what will probably happen after reading this column. As a parent, you'll catch your self saying one of these five things. That's natural. Sometimes it takes conscious attention to change. Simply stop your self, remember what your are trying to teach, and use one of the suggested alternatives. Or better yet, create your own.

ACTION QUESTIONS

1) Do you recognize yourself in any of these top five?
2) If so, what can you begin to do to change the pattern?

What Parents & Teens Say
About Each Other

"When I was your age........" **Any parent**
"You just don't understand....." **Any kid**

Helping to bridge the gap between teens and parents can get pretty tricky sometimes. At times it feels like I'm walking a tightrope between an angry lion and wise but bewildered elephants.

Over the years I've asked both parents and kids to write their answers to the following questions: "What's the hardest thing about being the parent of a teenager or a teenager?" What's the best thing about being the parent of a teenager or a teenager?" "What are some things you wish parents understood about teenagers or teenagers understood about parents?"

As you might imagine, there have been some interesting answers over the years. Some insightful, some heartbreaking, and some delightful. Here's a brief sampling out of the mouths of teenagers and parents.

The hardest thing about being a teenager is........

☞ having people that don't understand you trying to control you
☞ parents not understanding the things you have to deal with
☞ having to deal with school
☞ being accepted by friends
☞ having someone real close leave you
☞ being blamed for almost everything because we are teenagers

- living with divorced parents and having no say so in where you go
- dealing with boy\girl friends
- trying to deal with a parent who doesn't want to understand and take time to listen to your comments
- not being financially independent
- parents expectations and never being enough
- knowing your parents are right

The best thing about being a teenager is........

- getting away with immature behavior
- the chance to try new things
- having your whole life ahead of you
- youth, energy, time
- lots to look forward to
- getting a drivers license
- almost being done with school
- friends and relationships
- don't have to work
- summer vacation

Things I wish my parents understood about teenagers......

- our schedules and our social lives
- not knowing where my books are
- that restrictions don't work and talking does
- we're old enough to make our own choices
- we need to have our freedom every once in a while
- that we make mistakes just like they did
- grades aren't the only thing I'm good for, I can make you proud by just being me!!
- we love you even if you aren't around
- threats make me fear you, not respect you

☞ what the world is like now not what it was like when they were kids
☞ we have feelings too
☞ their words can hurt really bad
☞ it really is hard to live in a family where your opinion doesn't count
☞ that we understand trust isn't cheap but we have to learn some things for ourselves

The hardest part of being the parent of a teenager is.............

☞ letting them learn from their mistakes
☞ trying not to fix their problems
☞ we hurt when they hurt
☞ being lied to
☞ trying to continue to discipline
☞ having the consequence "fit the crime"
☞ hearing " you don't understand" over and over when in fact you really do or want to
☞ letting them make more of their own decisions

The best part about being the parent of a teenager is...........

☞ more time for myself since they can take care of themselves more
☞ learning, growing, changing and developing with them
☞ watching them grow and mature
☞ guiding them in decisions
☞ feeling proud of and sharing in their accomplishments
☞ hearing "I love you Mom/Dad"
☞ knowing they will be adults someday who don't live in my house

Something I wish teenagers understood about parents is........

☞ we try to do what we think is best for the child
☞ we have other things in life we want to do besides what the child wants to do
☞ parents sometimes make mistakes
☞ sometimes we forget or change our minds
☞ how much we love them
☞ parents want to keep kids from getting hurt, physically and emotionally
☞ we have feelings and needs too
☞ we are the adults
☞ I feel a responsibility to teach him how to take care of himself when he is on his own
☞ although things may be different now, we have gone through some of the same pressures and challenges and want to understand and be there for them
☞ we have a vision for your future and what you can be
☞ we still love you just as much when you make mistakes
☞ we get angry when we are disappointed
☞ how much of a challenge being your parent is
☞ we want respect
☞ we want them to have a better life and not have to work as hard as we do
☞ understand the stress that comes with the enormous responsibility of parenthood

So there we are. Some insights from both sides. When setting out to build bridges between parents and teens, it's crucial to remember that each side has valid viewpoints as well as something to learn from each other. And if parents are lucky, they get to live long enough to see their own kids have teenagers.

ACTION QUESTIONS

1) What is something you wish you understood about your teenager?
2) What is something you wish your teenager understood about you?
3) Now, with these questions and answers is hand, go have a conversation with your teenager.

Trust or Bust: It's Not All or Nothing

"Mom, can I go to the mall with my friend Jenny?
No, not after you came home late last night.
Well everybody else gets to.
I don't care what everybody else gets to do, you can't
You just don't trust me
You've got to earn it
I have
no you haven't
have too
have not"
SLAM!!! etc.

If the above conversation sounds familiar, you're probably the parent of a teenager. I especially love the "everybody else gets to do it" line. My parents response to that was "if everybody else stood on their head in the middle of the street at 3am in their underwear, would you?" Probably would have.

I never understood what all that meant; but I do know that raising teenagers can be an extremely challenging task. I have a tremendous amount of respect for the parents of the teenagers I work with in my practice. Now don't get me wrong. Most teenagers are pretty OK people. The vast majority seem to stay out of the juvenile justice system and eventually become adults. It's just that most of the teenagers I've worked with are 16 going on 26 and 16 going on 6, all at the same time.

There is a proverb that goes something like "raise a child in the way they should go and when they are old they won't depart from it". What that implies is at some point they are going to go away from it. Some families seem to go through the passage of the teen years with little or no struggle. Many other families find it one of the most challenging and at times,

75

maddening stages for their family. Parents of teenagers really try hard to navigate these difficult waters. One of the areas that seem to be the most difficult for parents is the issue of trust. Let's take a closer look at how trust operates in families with teenagers, how it sometimes gets damaged, and how it can be built back.

A few families seem to go along and never have any problems with or damage done to the trust level for their kids. Others can really struggle with this issue. One of the places families tend to get stuck is seeing trust as an either/or situation. The teen lies, breaks curfew, experiments with drugs, or something equally trust damaging. The parents feel like they have lost all trust in their teen. The problem, or the "sticking point", here is how do you build the trust back from nothing? How do we set it up so kids can earn back trust? Viewing trust as a matter of degree can help create a map back to a trusting relationship.

Here's an example of building a map back to trust as well as creating the structure to earn trust back. Let's say the teen has broken curfew by a few hours. The first step is looking at trust on a scale of 1 to 10, 1 is the least amount of trust, 10 is the most. Let's say that coming home late reduced the trust level from a 9 down to a 3. That's a gap of 6 trust levels. Creating a map back to a high trust level will be difficult if you try to go from a three to a nine all at once. It's just too big a leap.

The next step is to talk about and agree on what changes and/or behaviors need to occur to go from a three level to a four level; then from a four to a five; a five to a six; and so on. In this way several positive structures are set up. The parents have a way of monitoring their teens progress and the teen has something to work toward. In addition, there's a built in incentive for the teen. In many families, trust is kind of like playing video games at the mall. In the video arcade, the more tokens you have, the more you can play. In much the same way, in families, the more trust you have, the more you can do.

At this stage many parents will ask "How do I know things are really different, that I'm not getting fooled?" That's an excellent question and the best answer I can offer is simply to watch and see if the behavior matches the words. If it does, you're on the right track. If the behavior doesn't match the words, then you know someone trying to pull the wool over your eyes.

Trust is a crucial element during the sometimes difficult time of the teen years. If damage to trust occurs, first, remember that this is a common, although serious, occurrence. Second, begin building the road back to a trusting relationship. If you find yourself still stuck along the road, it may be time to call in some outside help in order to get unstuck. And one last thing - the teen years do come to an end, and if you are really lucky, you get to live long enough to watch your children have teenagers too!

ACTION QUESTIONS

1) What's the current level of trust in your family?
2) What can you begin to do immediately to improve the level of trust?

Building a "Parenting Team"

"Who's side are you on anyway?"

Any parent

Question: My spouse and I can not agree on how to raise our kids. I think my spouse is too strict and my spouse thinks I am too lenient. Meanwhile, the kids are getting away with everything. What can we do?

Answer: This is an excellent, and all too common question. So, in typical therapist fashion, I'm going to begin to answer the question with a question. Where in the world did we get the idea that two parents have to agree on every aspect of parenting? Somehow we are supposed to believe that two separate individuals, who grew up with different models of how to parent (if they had models at all), different life experiences, and probably different temperaments, are now going to come together and agree on every facet of the complicated task of parenting. Sorry, I just don't buy it.

Not only is this an unworkable notion in the real world, I believe it can be a damaging one as well. The optimal goal, of course, would be for these two different people to combine their respective parenting styles into a well functioning and supportive parenting team. In the best of situations, this is difficult, although it can, and does happen. When people believe the lie about always having to agree, it can set up a power struggle between the two adults.

We all like to be right and we tend to fight for our position. In too many situations, what happens is instead of coming together as a parenting team, the parents grow further and further apart, rigidly adhering to their own style. A person with a more strict style has something to learn from the person

78

with a more lenient style, and vice versa. Instead of learning from each other, the strict one becomes more strict and the lenient one becomes more lenient. This creates, at best, the following problems:
* it breeds criticism and resentment
* the children suffer
* the parents cancel each other out
* and it leaves a gap big enough for a child to drive a truck through

It also sets up what I call the "parent trap." Picture, if you will, a circular clock face. At twelve o'clock is the word ANGRY, at four o'clock is the word SYMPATHY, and at eight o'clock is the phrase, TAKEN ADVANTAGE OF. The trap begins when a child misbehaves, does something wrong or gets in trouble. The parent starts at the top of the clock, becomes ANGRY, and says something like, "OK, that does it, you are grounded for life!!!!" Or some equally realistic statement. After awhile, the parent moves on down the clock to SYMPATHY, and lets the child off the hook. Sure enough, the child takes advantage, and does the same thing, or something else equally frustrating. This moves the parent over to feeling TAKEN ADVANTAGE OF. The parent doesn't feel this way for too long before thinking or saying, "How could you do this after all I've done for you!?!" The parent quickly returns to the top of the clock and ANGER.

Do you see the vicious cycle this sets up? In the middle is the child, running the show. Now let's complicate this process even more with our two different parenting styles. Imagine having one parent stuck on anger and the other one stuck on sympathy, or some equally damaging combination. There's that hole you can drive a truck through I mentioned earlier.

There are many useful ways to get out of this parent trap. One of the simplest is called the odd/even schedule. Here's how it works. On odd numbered days, one parent will be in charge of parenting. That means that all discipline, privileges, discussions, etc. go through that parent for that entire day. The other parent is to stand by and merely observe (unless there is blood or some other legitimate emergency). The parent who is on for that day can call on the other parent as a consultant if they so choose. Otherwise, the off parent is required to "sit on their wisdom" for the day. On the next day, the even day, the roles are simply reversed. The parent who was is charge is off, and the parent who was off is in charge.

This plan can benefit the parents and the family in several ways:
- the parents come together to agree to follow the plan
- each parent gets to see the other one in action and see that they can parent
- each parent gets to practice their own parenting skills
- the children get to see each parent being in charge
- it opens the door for the parents to come together as a parenting team

The task of parenting is difficult enough without it becoming a power struggle between the two adults. It's crucial to remember that the goal is to form an effective parenting team, with both parents drawing on their own unique skills and learning from each other. In this way, every one benefits, the parents and the children.

ACTION QUESTIONS

1) In what ways do you currently find yourself in the parent trap?
2) What will it take to get out?
3) What will it take to stay out?

The Teenager and the Gorilla

"Why can't they be like we were, perfect in every way?"
Lee Adams, Bye Bye Birdie

Q: A parent writes in to ask, "You write a lot about the difference between controlling and managing teenagers. What's the difference........., and how do we do it in our family?"
A: In the counseling and seminars that I do, I have found that many parents are confused about the difference between controlling and managing their teenagers. In my experience, there is not only a huge difference, it's "the difference that makes a difference" when it comes to successfully dealing with the teen years in a family.

Taking a control approach in a family will typically breed resentment and rebellion in a teenager, and exasperation and anger on the part of the parents. While the control approach may get compliance, it also breeds an attitude of "I'll do what you say now, but I'm going to get you back someday." Coming from a management approach breeds respect and cooperation, as well as an attitude of "let's work together as a team." As I have said before, trying to control a teenager is like trying to put pants on a gorilla - it's only going to frustrate you and make the gorilla mad.

Now in no way am I saying that teens should be allowed to do whatever they want. The difference between trying to control vs. manage a teenager is all in how you approach the situation. A management approach meets the following six criteria:
♦ 1) The parents are clearly in charge.

When I work with parents to take a management approach with teens, in no way am I suggesting that parents let kids do whatever they want. Quite the contrary, a key sign of a healthy

81

and strong family is when the parents are clearly in charge. The key distinction comes down to the difference between an authoritarian style and an authoritative style on the part of the parents. An authoritarian style comes from a controlling approach, while an authoritative style comes from a management approach.

A good example of an authoritarian style can be found in the movie The Great Santini. This family was ruled by the iron hand of the father, a military man, who tried to run his family like he ran his troops, complete with morning inspections. The best example I've been able to find of an authoritative style is The Huxtables of The Cosby Show. If you think back to the show or watch the re-runs, you will notice that in the Huxtable family, the parents are clearly in charge. At the same time, there is compassion and caring for all the family members. One strong indication of this is that while each child may not always get a vote, they almost always have a voice.

♦ 2) The teen, over time, learns and earns the ability to be more and more in charge of themselves.

Notice I said *over time*. This simply means that the parents give the kid enough rope, not to hang themselves, to coin a phrase, but *to grow themselves*. You don't hand someone who has had little or no responsibility a huge responsibility all at once. You give them a little bit, and then a little bit more, and so on and so on.

♦ 3) There is a clear map for continually building trust and responsibility.

In a management approach, there is no guessing on the part of parent or kid. Everyone knows how trust and responsibility are earned in the family. The rules are clear with little or no surprises.

♦ 4) The parents have a way to monitor the progress of the teen.

One way to do this is to simply measure trust on a scale from 1 to 10. In this way, the parents have a clear and objective way of monitoring the progress of their teenager.

♦ 5) There are clear consequences when the teen demonstrates that they cannot be in charge of themselves (just like in the real world).

There is a proverb that goes something like this "raise up a child in the way they should go and when they are old they will not depart from it." What this implies is that at some point along the way, they are going to depart from it. It's simply part of the territory that kids are going to mess up. *Before* this happens, there needs to be a simple understanding about what will happen when the mess ups occur.

♦ 6) There is a clear map for how to earn back trust and responsibility.

Many parents tend to look at trust as an either or situation - either you trust them completely or not at all. Using a scale from one to ten not only gives parents a way to monitor progress, it can provide a map for how to earn trust back when it is damaged.

Successfully steering a family through the teen years is one of the most difficult jobs a parent will ever face. Using the six point management approach can help parents to get their kids, and themselves, through the adolescent years with most of their sanity intact.

ACTION QUESTIONS

1) Do you have a control or management approach in your home?

2) What would it take to switch to a management approach, and what might be the benefits?

Take a Management Approach with Teens

*"Trying to control a teenager is like
trying to put pants on a gorilla."*

Jef Herring

Q: We are having increasing difficulty dealing with curfews in our home. Our teenagers keep wanting to stay out later and later and it's hard for us to trust them. What can we do?
A: Isn't it amazing how kids believe that they can have fun only after a certain time of evening (or early morning)?

Curfew can be an area ripe for power struggles, conflict & frustration. When the subject of curfew comes up, many parents hear the same old refrains, "Every one else's parents let them stay out as long as they want" (check it out, it's probably not accurate), "All the fun happens after midnight", "C'mon mom, it's the 90's!", (your point?) & "When I get to be a parent, I'm going to let my kids stay out as late as they want" (right).

If not handled properly, curfew can become a battle ground with the parents playing warden to the teenage inmates, and kids sneaking out and/or not coming home in order to "prove" their independence.

Curfew can also be an area that can illustrate for us a useful model for managing the teenage years. Many times when a parent phones me about their teenager, they say something like "I can't seem to control my kid." What I find myself wanting to say is that may be the problem, trying to control vs. manage the situation. A parent trying to control a teenager is like trying to make a gorilla wear pants, it's only going to frustrate you and make the gorilla angry.

As children grow from the childhood years into the passage of adolescence, it's important for parents to remember what

84

the purpose of parenting and the purpose of adolescence is all about. Parenting is one of those rare jobs where one of the primary goals is to work yourself out of a job. One way this is done is by teaching the adolescent how to be more and more in charge of themselves. Interestingly enough, one of the major jobs of adolescents is to learn how to be more and more in charge of themselves.

Now in no way am I saying that teens should be allowed to do whatever they want. As a matter of fact, there are times when teens need more attention and structure than do younger children. The difference between trying to control vs. manage a teenager is all in how you approach the situation.

A management approach meets the following six key criteria:

- 1) the parents are clearly in charge
- 2) the teen, over time, learns and earns the ability to be more and more in charge of themselves
- 3) there is a clear map for continually building trust and responsibility
- 4) the parents have a way to monitor the progress of the teen
- 5) there are clear consequences when the teen demonstrates that they cannot be in charge of themselves (just like in the real world)
- 6) there is a map for how to earn back trust and responsibility.

Having said all that, allow me to more precisely answer your question about curfew. A solution I have seen work with many families, and that meets the six criteria of management vs. control is what I call the "Enough rope to grow yourself" solution.

In this solution, the parents choose a beginning place to start the curfew, let's say, for the sake of our example 10pm. If the teen is able to keep that curfew, (and I mean keep - no five or ten minutes late) for a certain period of time, let's say, again for the sake of our example, six months, the curfew can be extended another fifteen or thirty minutes. If at any time during the six month period the teenager breaks curfew, the six month period begins all over again.

The numbers here are just for example, you can change them to fit your own unique situation.

Checking this out with the six criteria for managing teenagers we see that the parents are clearly in charge, the teen has a way to earn more responsibility and trust, the parents have a way to monitor progress, consequences are clear, and there is a map for re-building trust and responsibility when it is damaged.

The passage of adolescence can be difficult enough without a never ending power struggle for control. Taking a management approach can go a long way to helping parents work themselves out of a job and grow the teenager into a well functioning young adult.

ACTION QUESTIONS

1) How did your parents handle the teen years?
2) How is your style the same and how is it different?
3) What about your style would need to change to more closely match a management style?

Deciding on Discipline Can Be a Punishing Task

"Every jail has to have a jailer."

Q: A parent writes in to ask, " We are having a hard time in our family deciding on appropriate punishments when our teenager breaks family rules. We can't tell if we are too strict or too lenient. What can we do?"

A: I'm glad you asked this question, because it seems to be a place where many parents get stuck. Questions about appropriate punishment and consequences are very important.

Now notice, if you will, that I just said punishment *and* consequences, not just punishment. This is because I believe there is an important distinction to be made between punishment and consequences. The difference has to do with what our goal may be in responding to unacceptable and inappropriate behavior. If our goal is to vent our anger, control a teenager and provoke resentment, then punishment is the way to go. If, on the other hand, our goal is to send a clear message, manage and guide a teenager, and instruct about life then consequences are the way to go.

The purpose of consequences for behavior is to teach about the real world. There are basically two kinds of consequences, natural and logical. Natural consequences occur naturally as a result of behavior and choices. In the adult world, if we run red lights, we can get hit and hurt; if we don't show up for work without a reason, we can get fired.

In the world of kids, there are times when allowing natural consequences to occur is much too dangerous. A parent should never allow to occur the natural consequences of running into a busy street, for example.

When natural consequences are too dangerous to allow to occur, it's time for the creation of logical consequences. In general, they involve some loss of privilege as a result of irresponsible behavior.

There are two general models that I use when it comes to structuring appropriate logical consequences. The first is a model designed by Stephen Glenn, the author of "How to Raise Self-Reliant Children in a Self-Indulgent World" (Prima Publishing, $10.95) that involves the Three R's of Logical Consequences - Related, Respectful, and Reasonable.

Let's take a look at each of these criteria.

- Related - Related simply means related to the behavior. If a child violates curfew, making them stay after school or cut the grass is not related. The temporary loss of the privilege of going out is related.
- Respectful - We need to avoid two things here. The first is putting down the teenager and the second is inconveniencing the adult.
- Reasonable - "You are grounded for life and will never see the light of day again" is unreasonable. "Your behavior and choices have caused you to lose the privilege of going out tomorrow night" is reasonable.

I have found Glenn's model to be very useful in my work with families. In addition to the Three R's of Consequences, I've added the The Three S's - Strong, Swift and Short-term.

Let's take a closer look at these criteria as well.

- Strong - The *intention* of the strength of a consequence is to get their *attention*. "Honey, I really wish you wouldn't come in so many hours after your curfew" is not strong. Losing the privilege of going out on the very next opportunity is strong.

The next two criteria have to do with the differences between adults and teenagers in their perception of time. As adults, if we are told a project is due in two months, we know we need to get moving yesterday. For many teens, two months equals eternity which equals no motivation.

- Swift - In order for consequences to be effective, they need to be closely linked in time to the misbehavior. For teenagers, not being able to go on a trip six months from now for flunking a test is ineffective. Having to spend extra time the next three days studying and therefore losing the privilege of afternoon free time is swift and effective.

- Short-term - When I was 13 years old, my parents grounded me for life. (If you want to find out why, come to a seminar!) In order for logical consequences to be effective, they need to be relatively short term. Again, this goes back to the issue of time. For most teenagers, anything past a few days or weeks (as long as the consequence is strong and swift) becomes ineffective. Anything longer breeds resentment, contempt and revenge, and loses the value of any life lessons that might be taught.

The purpose of parenting teens is to prepare them for life on their own in the real world. Using the R's and S's of Consequences can allow the parents to be in charge while teaching the lessons of life.

ACTION QUESTIONS

1) What's the difference between punishment and consequences?

2) How can you implement the three R's of consequences in your family?

3)) How can you implement the three S's of consequences in your family?

Ending Power-struggles with Your Teenagers

"Dodge trucks are ram tough"
Old commercial

Q: We keep getting into power-struggles with our teenager. Even when we win it feels like we all lose. What can we do differently without backing down?

A: That's another excellent and often asked question. I think you are right on target when you say that it feels like everyone loses, even when you "win." Most power-struggles between parents and teenagers are a "lose/lose" proposition.

Remember the commercial a few years back that had the two rams repeatedly butting heads on top of a mountain? The slogan was "Dodge trucks are ram tough!" Even though they have horns to butt heads with, it always looked to me like it really hurt. I believe it's the same way when parents and teens butt heads.

Where in the world did we get the idea that the parent-teen relationship is a struggle in which one side has to win and the other side lose? One of the greatest sources of power struggles is the belief that not only does each side have to win each battle, they have to battle over each and every issue that arises. The parent has bought into the mistaken belief that they always have to "win" in order to be good parents. In the passion, exuberance and "wisdom" of youth, the teen believes that every battle is a fight for independence that must be won, at all costs. It's like the lyric from the Elton John song "Bennie and the Jets"; "We'll fight our parents out in the street to find out who's right and who's wrong." Most parents wind up feeling like the line from the Harry Chapin song "Tangled-up Puppet"; "Don't you know that you don't need to grow up all alone?"

One of the easiest breeding grounds for power struggles seems to be the whole issue of school and grades. Here's how I think it works. The parents view is that they work all day and the kids don't. Therefore school is the child's job and they should make great grades. The kids view is that school is their social world interrupted by six or seven classes a day.

The alternative is learning to pick your battles. Now in no way am I suggesting that parents back down and let the teen win. I'm simply suggesting that you decide what the important issues are and go from there. For example, it was amazing to me when I was a director of a drug treatment center for teens how quickly parents would go from almost losing their kid to drugs to complaining about them not making their bed or cleaning their room. I think Ann Landers has it right when she says that sometimes the best solution to a messy room is a closed door.

When my wife and I were planning our wedding, I learned a great deal about picking your battles. I wanted the wedding to be in Tallahassee and she wanted it to be in Orlando/Winter Park where we both grew up. The wedding was held in Orlando. This was my first lesson in how much say the groom gets in planning the wedding. It's like the old joke - "It takes two people to plan a wedding - the bride and her mother." One other important thing I learned was that even if you care not about some of the details, it's crucial to act like you do. "Of course I care about the color of the napkins at the reception!"

Anyway, there were two or three things in the wedding that were very important to me, such as the music. I saved my battles for those things that were the most important to me.

In my experience, it works the same way for parents and teenagers as well.

After you have picked your battles and chosen what's important, here's a simple four step formula for creatively handling power struggles called "Developing Your Parent's Playbook."

♦ 1) Identify the situation that has become a power-struggle.

♦ 2) Identify two or three solutions that you have tried that don't work. Even if they "should" work, or they worked for your parents, or they worked for your other child, or you read in some article that they worked. If it doesn't work, it doesn't work!

♦ 3) Come up with absurd, ridiculous, creative, outlandish ideas that you would never do, but are fun and a good laugh to just think and talk about. This is sort of like David Letterman's line "Kids, don't try this at home!"

By the time a situation reaches the level of a power-struggle, the parents have usually lost their sense of humor and the situation has become what I call "deadly dull." The parents have lost their ability to think creatively and are simply and painfully stuck. Suggesting they be creative is useless unless you show them how. Coming up with ridiculous and absurd solutions allows parents to laugh and get enough perspective to be creative. It's also a lot of fun!

♦ 4) Create useful, alternative solutions (UASs). Sometimes the seeds for a UAS are in the ridiculous ideas. Other times simply being able to laugh, step back and get perspective allows for the creation of useful alternatives.

ACTION QUESTIONS

1) What is your contribution to the current power struggles?
2) How could you apply your "parent's playbook" to current situations at home?

The Sport of Parenting:
Creatively Solving Power Struggles

"The moment you enter in to a power struggle
with your teenager, you have already lost"

Jef Herring

Q: "We are continually faced with escalating power struggles
with our 16 year old son. No matter what we try to do, it
seems he has to fight us for all he is worth. When we fight
back harder to try to make him do what we want, it just seems
to make matters worse and worse. We don't want to give in,
but we are afraid of what might happen next. Do you have any
suggestions for how we can successfully make a stand without
losing the relationship?"

A: You have asked a very good question, one that almost
every family with teenagers has to confront at some point.

Let's start with a general rule about power struggles and
teenagers. Once you enter into a power struggle with a
teenager, you have already lost. Not because they are more
powerful than parents. Not at all. It's simply that once you
enter into a power struggle, you may end up winning, but you
only get to do so at the expense of the relationship.

Am I saying that parents are to back off and just let the
teen do whatever they what? Not on your life! Or theirs for
that matter. What I am saying is that as parents, you have to
work smarter instead of harder. The first step involves a shift
in your focus.

Here's what I mean. Simply stated, the shift involves
moving from deciding what you are going to try to make your
teen do to focusing on what you are going to get yourself to
do as parents.

So how do we do that? The second step involves a four step process that helps you to creatively solve parent-teen difficulties, and have fun doing it. I realize that's a fairly bold statement. Read on and see what you think.

I call this four step process Developing Your Parent's Playbook. It's one of my favorite skills to teach at seminars. Let's take a look at each of the four steps and then use a real life example.

- Step 1 - Identify the problem situation.
- Step 2 - Identify one or two solutions you have tried that don't work, even though it seems like they should work. This is where most parents get stuck. They keep on doing the same things that don't work over and over again and expect different results. It may have worked before, it may have worked on another child, or some guy in a column said it would work. The bottom line is this - if it's not working, it's not working, and it's time to try something different.
- Step 3 - Here's the fun part. Come up with creative, ridiculous, absurd, crazy and outlandish ideas, _that you would never do,_ but are just fun to think about and get you laughing.

Here's what happens. Power struggles become so deadly dull serious that we lose our sense of humor and therefore our creativity. The purpose of step three is to allow you to step back from the problem just a bit and laugh, so you can use your own creativity. I am always amazed at the natural creativity of parents in solving problems.

- Step 4 - Come up with creative, alternative solutions. Sometimes the seeds for solutions are in the crazy ideas from step three. Other times, parents are able to find solutions they couldn't see before.

Now let's move from the theoretical into the practical and use a real life example from a recent seminar.

- Step 1 - The problem - 20 year old son comes home at all hours of the night, if at all, greatly disrupting the household.
- Step 2 - Attempted solutions that don't work - grounding him and taking the car away.
- Step 3 - Creative-crazy solutions - these parents and the seminar group came up with several elegantly absurd ideas, the best of which follows. The next time he came home in the wee hours of the morning, their son would find the locks changed, in the front yard a small tent erected for him under a flashing neon sign that said, "Here lies our grown son who came home too late one too many times."

Now remember, this is not something they would do, but they sure had fun thinking about it.

Also remember, the point of this exercise is not to make the son do anything. The point is for the parents to decide what they are going to do and to control what they can control, which is themselves. That leads us to the creative alternative solutions.

- Step 4 - Here's what these parents came up with as a creative solution to take home. They would begin to treat their son like the adult he wanted to be, beginning with posting a new address on his bedroom door. If their street address was 2908, his address would become 2908 1/2. This was to signify that he was now an adult, with adult privileges *and* adult responsibilities, such as cleaning your own room and clothes, making your own meals and paying rent, to name just a few.

Last time I checked with these folks, the creative solutions were working, and they were sleeping at night.

Parent-teen power struggles are no fun. Using your Parent's Playbook can go a long way to solving problems and preserving the relationship. I invite you to see what your own natural creativity can accomplish in your family.

ACTION QUESTIONS

1) How do you get hooked into power struggles with your teens?

2) If you haven't already done so, go back now and practice your parent's playbook.

Family Conflict: Voices and Votes

"You never listen to me"

Another teenager

Q: A parent writes in "We are having war at our house trying to talk with our teenage daughter. Whenever we try to communicate why we don't think she should do something, she screams "You never listen and you never understand! I hate you!" How can we deal with this!?

A: Thanks for writing in. These kind of impasses are common between parents and teenagers. Fortunately, there are several useful solutions that I can offer.

In doing family therapy with adolescents for the past 20 years, I've come across this impasse time and time again. Here is a list of four things parents can do to get past this stuck place.

- 1) A starting place is for parents to realize the trap that is being set when their kids asks, "Well, why can't I (fill in the blank)." Many well intentioned parents then proceed to give a well reasoned response to the question and then wonder why the kid blows up and doesn't accept it at all.

Here's a response I believe a parent will never get - "Thank you for that explanation Mom and Dad, I've never thought of it that way before. And now that you have explained it that way, I not only can't believe I wanted to do that, I apologize for asking. Thanks for setting me straight."

Yet as parents we act as if that is the response we expect. Most of the time, no explanation will suffice. Sometimes "because we said so" is the most useful and appropriate response.

- 2) When kids yell "You never listen to me and you just don't understand" and the parents say "Yes we do!", they are talking about two different things. They are simply "not on the same page" when it comes to their definition of listening and understanding.

Many times, when a teenager says you just don't understand or listen to me, what they are really saying is you are not agreeing with me and I'm mad and I'm going to try and get my way!

The solution here is for the parents to make it clear that while in their family they "will almost always get a voice, they won't always get a vote."

Taking this position exposes the game the kid is playing and helps to put the parents in charge.

- 3) Hearing the words "I hate you!" is one of the most painful things for parents to experience. It doesn't help that the words are not spoken softly and are often screamed at them. Being able to see what I'm about to say can be very difficult, but it doesn't make it any less true. When a kid yells "I hate you!", many times they are not talking to you but to themselves. Adolescence is a tremendously hard time for some kids, filled at times with low self esteem, self contempt and loathing. Unfortunately, their anger and frustration is misdirected and comes out at the parents, resulting in "I hate you" statements.

It's important to point out that this doesn't make it acceptable to say. It's not. It just exposes what is really happening here.

- 4) There is a very common trap here into which many parents fall. It's the trap of trying to make your teenager see or do something a certain way, usually the way you think it should be done. The more you try to convince them to do it your way, the more they are committed to doing it their way. Just as in most traps, the more you aimlessly struggle, the more trapped you become and the harder it is to get out.

A very useful technique for getting out of this trap is offered to us by Jane Nelson and Lynn Lott, in their book, "Positve Discipline for Teenagers" (Prima Publishing, $14.95). Nelson and Lott focus on the need for parents of teens to *stop* deciding what they are going to make their kid do and *start* deciding what they are going to do. This puts the parents back in charge by giving them control over something they can have control over - namely themselves.

For our example here, this would involve deciding what is acceptable and unacceptable, and then sticking with it. It's really OK for your teenager not to like it. That's often part of being a teenager.

In closing, I want to re-emphasize the importance of letting them know that while they almost always have a voice, they just won't always get a vote. In the meantime, stick around long enough to enjoy watching your kids have their own teenagers!

ACTION QUESTIONS

1) What does it mean to give a teen a voice?
2) What does it mean to give a teen a vote?
3) How does it work in your family?

The Parent's Job & the Teen's Job

16yo teenager: *"I want to go out with my friends tonight, OK!?!*
Parent*: "No , not tonight, you went out last night."*
Teen: *"So, I still want to go"*
Parent: *"I don't care, I said no!"*
Teen: *"Well, I don't care what you say, I'm still going!"*
Parent: *"NO YOU ARE NOT!!"*
Teen: *"YES I AM!!!"*   Slam!!

Ah, the joys of parent-teen power struggles. In the twenty years I've been working with teenagers and their families, I've heard many variations of the above power struggle. I often find myself saying something like this to the family, "As parents it's your job to set limits and to say no at times. As a teenager, it's your job to rebel, pull away and try to turn no into a yes. It looks to me as if both of you are doing your jobs really well."

Having said that, just what are the jobs of parent and teenager? Let's take a closer look at these differing, and often times, conflicting jobs. In addition, we'll look at some "job tips" for each one.

♦   The Teen's Job

Part of the teen's job is to begin to break away, defining themselves in ways separate from the family. This means they begin to pull away from the family and move toward the peer group. In developmental terms, this is very normal. It can also be very noisy.

Optimally, while the teen is defining him- or herself as different from their family, they are also learning to be more and more in charge of themselves. Remember the TV sitcom "Family Ties"? The Keatons were the laid back, grew up in the '60's parents, while their son Alex was the ultimate yuppie and

Reagan-loving Republican. A good example of defining self as different from the family.

♦ Tips for Teens
• Pick your battles. There's lots of ways to go through the teen years besides kicking and screaming. Every issue doesn't have to be a battle for independence.
• Treat your parents like guides instead of the enemy. Even though times are radically different, they have walked this way before. It was Mark Twain who said, " W hen I was a boy of 14, my father was so ignorant I could hardly stand to have him around. But when I got to be 21, I was astonished at how much he had learned in seven years. "
• Earn your parent's trust. In families, trust is like video games at the mall. With video games, the more tokens you have, the more you can play. In families, the more trust you have, the more you can do.

♦ The Parent's Job
Here's a story-metaphor that describes the parent's job. Last year as I painted our house, I watched a bird building a nest in the vines around our mailbox. Each day, the mother bird first brought twigs, and then moss and paper to soften the nest for the baby birds. As the days passed after the baby birds were born, (it took a long time to paint the house), I noticed that the mother bird began to remove the moss and paper, and soon after that the birds were flying and on their own, off to create their own families.

In this story we can see that the job of parents is to grow a successfully functioning person who can then leave the nest and create their own life out in the world.

♦ Tips for Parents
• Learn to pick your battles also. Every issue is not a contest of wills, or a definition of your worth as a parent.

- Give your kids enough rope, not to hang themselves, but to *grow themselves.*
- Set boundaries and limits from day one. If you don't set limits on toddlers and children, what in the world makes you think they will obey curfew when they are teenagers?
- In rough times, love them for who they are, not what they do.

"But how do we know if we are doing it right?", you might ask. A good question. In closing, I believe Robert Fulghum, author of "All I Ever Needed to Know I Learned in Kindergarten", has some wise words to offer us, "You will never really know what kind of parent you were, or if you did it right or wrong. Never. And you will worry about this and them as long as you live. But when your children have children and you watch them do what they do, you will have part of an answer."

ACTION QUESTIONS

1) What do you believe to be the parent's job?
2) What do you believe to be the teenager's job?
3) How does your family match these beliefs?

How to Have a Successful School Year

*"For the average teen, school is their social world
interrupted by six or seven classes a day"*

Jef Herring

Q: With the school year just beginning, what can we do as
parents to help make this a successful year for our teenager
and our family? Are there any specific things we can do?
A: Great question. Fortunately there are many things you can
do to make this a successful school year, not just for your teen,
but for the whole family as well.

In general, the first thing to keep in mind is that parents and
teens have a very different notion about the purpose of school.
Here's how I believe it works: For parents, the perception is
that we work all day, the kids don't. School is their job.
Therefore, they should get good grades, just as we want to do
well on our jobs.

The teenagers perception is quite different, however. In
their view, school is rarely more than their social world,
interrupted by six or seven classes a day.

Having said that, here's a list of the top seven things you as
a parent can do to make this a successful school year.

♦ Create an environment at home that models a love of
learning. How often have your children seen you reading?
Heard you talking about something you have learned?
Discussed ideas and issues with them? While these are
things to have started from day one with your child, you
can still implement them in your home now.

♦ In whatever way works for you, make sure your teen
knows that while grades are vitally important, they are
more important to you than their grades. That's the number

one thing I hear from kids when I ask them what gets in the way of talking about school with their parents.

♦ This one is so simple yet so profound. Ask them their opinion on important issues of the day. You may surprised to find out what kind of brain they have in there.

♦ Make sure there is nothing blocking your teenager from learning. One example of a block to learning could be a learning or information processing disorder, or something like Attention Deficit Disorder. Many teenagers I work with that have difficulty with school have undiagnosed ADD or ADHD.

Another block to learning can be the use of alcohol and drugs. Part of the process of drug abuse is that kids begin to lose interest in things that were once very important to them. If they are drunk or high in school, not only do they not want to learn, they can't.

♦ Know the names and philosophies of the following people who influence your child's life: the principal, assistant principles, the guidance counselor, and most especially the teachers.

♦ Take a walk through their school one day. By all means, don't let them see you. The reason I suggest this is parents need to understand at an experiential level that the school world their kids go to each day is nothing like the school world we knew. Not even close. Even if it's the same school. Just too much has changed.

♦ If discussion about grades has become a battleground during a particular time of day, declare that time "off limits" to grade talk, unless the teen brings it up. For some families that time is the care ride home, or right after school. For many it's the dinner table. Many families have reported better digestion after declaring dinner time off limits to grade talk.

Once you have done all this, simply put them in charge of school. What I mean by this is make them responsible for their performance at school. This may be particularly difficult, because this can be one of those situations where things may get worse before they get better. This is especially true if you have been pushing and pushing the last few years. There may be a drop off in performance as they learn how to be in charge of themselves with school.

Wanting your children to excel in school is a good and natural thing. There comes a time when the ball is simply in their court, and it's up to them. I think the most important thing for parents to remember is that school eventually needs to become more important to them than it is to you.

ACTION QUESTIONS

1) What do you believe to be the parent's job when it comes to school?

2) What do you believe to be the teen's job when it comes to school?

3) Now take these answers and go have a conversation with your teen.

Reflections on the First Year of Fatherhood: *No Pants!*

"Don't know much about you
Don't know who you are
Don't know why you chose us
Were you watching from above?
Is there someone there that knows us
Said we'd give you all our love?"

Marc Cohn 1993

Our son in one year old. *Our son. One year old.* These are words that I'm still trying to get my head around. From the moment he poked his tiny head out in to the world at 4am one Sunday morning, I've been hopelessly and helplessly in love with this kid.

The birth and delivery were rough, both mother and child were at risk. The most helpless feeling in the world is to see someone you love in pain and not being able to do a thing but be there and pray.

Later that morning, after calling everyone I could think of, I watched the sun come up, and felt like my whole entire world had changed forever.

"I'll promise you anything if you'll just go to sleep"

Bruce Carroll, 1993

Still feel that way. I have learned more in the last year about the depths of love that seem about to burst your heart, as well as how really well you can function on little or no sleep, for weeks at a time.

Lots of questions arise - what will he be like? Are we doing this right? This really lasts for 18 + years? Tell me again why we *wanted* to do this? Will he *ever* sleep through the night?

◆ 4AM on another morning

Not too long ago, our son was cutting teeth and not sleeping through the night again. Early one morning he woke up yelling at 4 am. First step - pick him up and rock him back to sleep. Nope, not this time. Second step - give him a bottle. Nope, not working either. Third step - take him for a drive. The only problem was I had just a t-shirt and underwear on, and both my pants and wallet were back in our bedroom. If I've learned anything in the past year, it's two things, 1) you never wake a sleeping baby, and 2) you never *ever* wake a sleeping mother! So in my 4am logic, I decided no one was going to see me, and we went for the drive. This time the reliable-works-every-time car ride didn't work. And, as you might have guessed by now, I got pulled over for speeding.

As I was pulling over I assessed the situation - it's 4:30am, I've got a screaming kid, no wallet, my wife's purse on the front seat, and *no pants* - and decided that I was so in jail.

The following conversation took place -

Me: "Officer, I'm sorry, I'm just trying to get my kid to sleep."

Officer: "At 60 mph on Capital Circle? Can I see your license and registration please?"

Me: "Well officer, we've got a problem, my license is about a mile around the corner from here and I'll be glad to get it for you."

Officer: "No it's too late for that." He proceeded to write down all the vital info to go and check me out. Then came the question I was dreading -

Officer: "Would you step out of the car please, sir?"

Me: "Well, officer, (while looking down at my bare legs), we've got another problem."

Officer: (Looking at me with a look that said he didn't know if he had a father or a pervert on his hands) "Are you telling me you are naked?"

Me: "No officer, I have on underwear, I was just trying to get my kid asleep." With a disgusted look, he walks back to his car, calls me in on the radio. Meanwhile I'm sitting there thinking that my wife is home asleep and has no idea what is happening with her son and husband.

Apparently the officer discovered I'm one of the good guys because he comes back to the car and tells me that all he is going to do is ticket me for driving without proof of license.

The conversation ended with -

Officer: "And next time, sir, I suggest you wear your pants."

Me: "Thank you, officer, I'll remember that."

It's really hard to imagine that this little guy who looks at me so lovingly now will be a teenager someday who thinks I'm an idiot. And with all the teens and families I've worked with over the years who might be watching, we'll probably just move out of town.

If parenthood is anything like being married, much of my professional clinical knowledge will go out the window when it comes to my own life. I guess we'll just do the very best we can, just like all the other families I've known through the years.

Happy birthday, son. I love you very much.

Marriage

Couples

Relationships

*"When you marry,
you don't marry
one person,
you marry three.
The person you think they are,
the person they really are,
and the person they will become
as a result of marrying you"*

Musings on Marriage

"Marriage, the final frontier"
Mad About You

In today's column I offer a collection of musings, observations and random (or rambling) thoughts on marriage and relationships, based on 20 years of doing marital counseling and my own life experience.

So here we go -

- W.C. Fields once said "When you marry, you hire a full time witness to your folly." One of the most interesting and humbling things about marriage is that our partner gets to see us at our absolute worst over and over again. When you think of it this way, it's amazing they stay with us at all.

- I've rarely seen a situation when one person is nagging without the other person being irresponsible in some way. They just seem to go together. I'm sure these words will come back to haunt me someday.

- Most people who come in for marriage counseling aren't sure if they want to be together or if they want to be apart, they just know for sure that they don't want the relationship to be like it is right now.

- Sometimes one spouse (usually the man) won't come to therapy because they "don't believe in counseling." My question to them is "Do you believe more in misery and divorce?"

- Research shows that 60% of all divorces can be traced back to difficulties with money. Each person comes to marriage with their own "money style", which is made up of the emotional meaning we give to money and the way money was handled in the family we grew up in. The successful blending of these two styles is the goal of successful couples.

- Here's another quote about marriage - "marriages are made in heaven, but so is thunder and lightning." In my seminars for couples, I always ask people if they get along 24/7 (that's 24 hours a day, 7 days a week for those of you who don't have teenagers). No one has ever raised their hand and I don't expect them to. It's normal and natural, even healthy, for two people who live under the same roof to disagree and even argue. Here's a suggestion for improving the way couples handle arguments. Ask yourself four key questions, 1) How do I handle anger?, 2) How would I like to handle it differently?, 3) How does my partner handle anger?, and 4) How would I like my partner to handle it differently?
- Being a marriage therapist doesn't guarantee a perfect marriage. I cringe every time someone says to my wife, "Oh you're so lucky to have a marriage counselor for a husband." I cringe because one day she'll tell them I'm just as big a jerk as anyone else.
- For most people, marriage is both the hardest thing they ever did *and* the smartest thing they ever did, all at the same time. And it's both the hardest and the smartest for the same reason - marriage causes us to grow in ways and deal with things that we never would have otherwise (or even wanted to, sometimes).
- There is a proverb that says "without a vision, the people perish." I believe this holds true for marriage as well. Yet the average couple spends more time planning a two week vacation than they do planning a marriage. What would it be like to ask the question, "If we could have it any way we wanted, how would we like this relationship to be?" That's the beginning of creating a vision for your relationship.

- Yet another quote about marriage, and I'll close with this one. "When you marry, you don't marry one person, you marry three. The person you think they are, the person they really are, *(here's the part that gets me)* and the person they will become as a result of marrying you."

The last part of that quote is a very sobering thing to think about. How often do we stop and think about our influence, *for better or worse,* on the person we have married? To put hands and feet on that question, I'll alter another famous quote by John Kennedy. "Ask not what this relationship or person can do for me, ask what I can do for this person and relationship." Perhaps that is one definition of love.

To wrap this up, my thanks go out to all the couples who have patiently taught me about what works and what doesn't. I genuinely appreciate your desire to grow, and your patience with me.

ACTION QUESTIONS

1) What actions might you need to take based on these musings?
2) What musings of your own could you add to this list?
3) What did you learn from your parents about marriage?
4) What do you want to keep, what do you want to get rid of?

Relationship Wounds

"In any marriage......there are grounds for divorce"
Robert Anderson

Playwright Robert Anderson is quoted as saying, "In any marriage of over 2 weeks duration, there are grounds for divorce. The trick is to find, & continue to find, grounds for marriage."

In even the very best of relationships, partners can hurt each other. When the pain becomes too great, the hurts become wounds. And many relationships have wounds. Any time you spend as much time with each other as a typical married couple does, there will most likely be wounds in the relationship at some time.

Just like physical wounds to the body, emotional wounds, left untreated, can cause infection or drain the life-blood out of a relationship.

There are several common and deadly relationship wounds. They usually reflect a lack of something in the relationship. Today we will look at three specific relationship wounds along with suggestions for how to treat them.

♦ Lack of Communication

Lack of communication is probably the most common as well as one of the most deadly. Communication serves to bring people closer together. When couples consistently fail to communicate, they slowly become strangers to each other. This is one of the main ways couples drift from soul mates to room mates.

Communication can be a really simple thing, yet we end up making it so hard. I'm a big believer in simple things, that anyone can do, so that when people do them, it has a profound effect.

So it is with something I call "Communication 101." So often in communication, we think we know what the other person means, we respond to that, they think they know what we mean, they respond to that, and we are off to the races, so to speak.

Really communicating, really listening to each other, involves both slowing the process down, and developing some skills. Here's a simple, yet profound, five step process to improving communication between couples.

Step 1 - Partner 1 talks about something.

Step 2 - Partner 2 says what they heard and then asks if they "got it."

Step 3 - Partner 1 then has three options. They can say "yes you got it", "you got that part, and you didn't get this part", or "no you didn't get it, that's not what I'm saying." You then repeat steps 1 - 3 until Partner 2 gets it.

Step 4 - After both people believe the message was received, partner 2 talks about what they think and how they feel about what was said. Now partner 1 repeats steps 2 and 3, until they get it. And so forth, and so on.

Does this feel awkward at first and slow the process down? Sure does. Does this help people communicate better and heal relationship wounds. You bet.

♦ Lack of Trust

Trust is part of the glue that holds couples together and provides a feeling of safety and security. When trust breaks down, people feel unsafe and insecure, and the glue begins to weaken.

To begin to build trust back after it has been weakened, you need to ask some questions. What does trust look like to you? What does it look like to your partner? What small things, if done on a regular basis, will begin to build and restore the weakened trust?

113

The answers to these questions can begin to give you a map for restoring trust and healing this relationship wound.

♦ Lack of Fun

I guess it could be said that "the couple that plays together, can stay together." Lack of fun is a wound sure to drain the passion and life out of any relationship. We get so caught up in the daily grind of jobs and bills and kids, etc. etc. When this happens, it becomes all to easy to get stuck in a rut and simply forget about having fun as a couple.

I've said this before and I'll say it again, because I think we need reminding - the only difference between a rut and a grave are the dimensions.

If you find yourself with this relationship wound, here's a simple way to heal it. Each of you write down ten things you would like to do for fun. Then each week, pick one item from your list and commit the time to doing it.

Some of you may be balking at this point, saying "We just don't have enough time together to do any of this." Perhaps, but allow me to get very serious with you for a moment. More than likely, one of you will die before the other one. What do you think the surviving partner will be saying at that point - "Boy, I wish we would have accomplished more" or "I wish we would have communicated more, trusted more, and had more fun."

OK, come back to the present. You are both still alive. You still have time to communicate, trust, and have fun. Now that I have your attention, I'll leave you to begin to heal these wounds. Keep the change.

ACTION QUESTIONS

1) What relationships wounds are you currently experiencing?
2) What are the first steps you will take to begin to heal them?

Voices of Experience Talk About Marriage

"Whatever is good for my wife is good for me"
A wise and experienced husband

Recently I was on a radio talk show out of New Orleans called "The Andre' Show" on WWL, discussing "What Makes a Marriage Successful". The producers had seen my column in the New Orleans paper and decided to create a talk show topic from the column. So now I'll create a column from the talk show. Are you with me so far? OK.

The format of the show was for the host and I to talk about what makes a successful marriage, my upcoming book, "The Seven Seeds for Growing a Healthy Marriage" and to take calls from the listening audience. We received dozens of calls from listeners on what had made their marriage successful, and we were not able to get to them all. I was on as the supposed "marriage expert." The real experts were the people calling in to offer what had made their marriage a success through the years.

Let's take a closer look at the themes and the advice of these experts on creating a successful marriage.

• Commitment

The strongest theme throughout all the calls was the notion of commitment, both to the other person and to the marriage. This came from callers who had been married anywhere from ten to fifty years. And these were not people who had stayed together "for the kids" or because it was the "right thing to do." These were people who seemed to actually be enjoying marriage and their partner after so many years.

Many of these callers spoke about how rough it was in the beginning. They each spoke about how it was their commitment that held them together through the early rough spots. As one caller stated, "The beginning can be rough, but staying through the tough times to get to the good times has definitely been worth it. Besides, it's what we said we would do in our vows."

- Shared problem-solving

One of the key factors that seemed to keep the commitment alive was the notion of shared problem-solving. One caller shared the traditional cliche "We just don't let the sun go down on our anger." My comment was that there might be many people who never got any sleep with that notion! But what the caller went on to say was this, "We don't have to think alike, we have just learned to think together". Excellent advice.

Another caller made this interesting distinction about arguing and problem solving - " We always make sure to argue as 'friends' and not as 'husband and wife.'" This one had me really curious, so I asked the caller two questions, 1) could they elaborate, and 2) could I use this notion in my work. They said yes, I could use it and went on to explain how when arguing, they focus on holding each other in the high esteem of a long time best friend, and not in the position of someone who is trying to beat them in an argument. The notion seems to work for them and also seems to be working in my office so far.

- Humor and Laughter

Many of the successful couples had found a way to use laughter and humor to keep the spark alive and move through some of the rougher waters. As one woman put it "we have learned to take our marriage seriously, but not ourselves." What an interesting notion.

- Putting your spouse first

One gentleman said that he believed that one of their secrets to success was that early on he decided that "whatever is good for my wife is good for me." Now the pop psychology of the '80's would say that this man is codependent, that is, too dependent on his wife, etc., etc. While there is a useful place for the notion of co- or over-dependency on someone, it's a notion that has been taken to an unhealthy extreme. Just think about it, you are "co-dependent" on the chair you are sitting in to read this book, for goodness sake. What I believe this couple has discovered is the power of "interdependency", the ability to trust and depend on each other. He sounded very happy, and I'm willing to bet his wife is pretty happy as well.

These are just a few of the themes that came out on the program. What I've come to believe is that the real experts are those folks out there who have created successful marriages. So here's a question - "What are the things that have made your marriage so successful?" What's the difference that makes the difference? Let us hear from you. After all, you're the real experts!

ACTION QUESTIONS

1) What actions could you take based on these insights?
2) What additional insights could you offer from your own experience?

Creating a Relationship Map

"Honey, where are we?"

Any spouse

Consider with me, if you will, the last vacation you were able to take. Whether a three day weekend or a full two week vacation, think back to all the planning that was involved. Things like where to go, what to take with you, notifying people you would be gone, and even consulting a map on how to get there. Quite a bit of preparation, conscious thought and planning goes into a successful vacation.

Now consider this - how much planning and conscious thought has gone into your marriage relationship?

I know, I know, I sort of set you up there, didn't I? It's just that it's truly amazing to me how some folks will spend more time planning a two week vacation than they do planning how they would like their marriage relationship to be.

In the theme song for the TV sitcom "Mad About You", marriage is called "the final frontier." Wouldn't it be nice if there was a way to create a map to guide us on our journey through the frontier of marriage? A marriage map could be especially useful in a culture where the most recent statistics (Family Therapy Networker, April/May '95) show that the average American couple spends just 20 minutes a day sharing together. Given this statistic, the lack of a "relationship map" can be deadly to a marriage.

Most of us seem to stumble into relationships and marriage, and then continue to kind of make it up as we go along. It's been my clinical experience that relationships take much more conscious planning to be successful. I guess if I was selling insurance I would be saying, " Most people don't plan to fail, they just fail to plan."

So how do you create a relationship map for your marriage? Actually, there are several different ways. One of the simplest and yet most profound is through the process of modeling. When you want to do something that you never have before, you don't have to reinvent the wheel. You simply find someone who has done or is doing what you want to do, discover what they have done or do, and simply do it as well.

This idea of modeling works so well because success leaves clues. In terms of marriage, look around in your own world for the couples who have the strongest and most enjoyable marriages. At this point you may be thinking there are not a whole lot of examples from which to choose. This may be true, but look around, they are out there. That doesn't mean they don't have their share of struggles. It just means they have found a way to manage them in a way that strengthens their marriage.

So how do you find out what their map has been to get them to where they are? Simple - just ask! While it may seem awkward at first, as I have interviewed and modeled different people, it's been my experience that most folks are honored to be asked and very willing to help.

Here are some questions to ask successful couples about how to build your own relationship map. Start out with general questions and then get more specific.

- What do you think has made your marriage so successful?
- What are the top five things that go into a healthy relationship?
- What do you have to believe about your spouse to keep your marriage strong?
- How do you handle small conflicts?
- How do you handle larger conflicts?
- How do you come to agreement about your finances?
- How do you come to agreement on how to handle the children?

- How do you divide domestic chores?
- What do you do on a daily basis to keep the spark alive?
- What has been your biggest challenge as a married couple? How did you handle it?
- Do you keep the toilet seat up or down?

These are just a sampling of the many questions you can ask successful couples. You can come up your own questions to help you create your own map. The most important factor is to simply ask.

Creating a map to guide you along the way can be very useful as you travel the frontier of marriage. And always remember to enjoy the journey!

ACTION QUESTIONS

1) Are you making it up as you go along/do you have a map?
2) What would a relationship map look like to you?
3) Do you hang the toilet paper over or under?

How to Get Out of "Relationship Ruts"

*"The only difference between a rut
and a grave are the dimensions"*

Q: My wife and I are both on our second marriage. We feel like we are both losing some of our excitement and love for each other, just like is our first marriages. We feel like we are stuck in a rut. What can we do to get out of this rut?
A: You've not only asked an excellent question, it's even been asked in song. In the song "Make Love Stay", by Dan Fogelberg, the song writer asks,

*"Now that we've loved,
Now that the lonely nights are over
How do we make love stay?"*

New relationships are exciting. The thrill of falling in love and discovering new things about each other is simply a lot of fun. After the honeymoon stage of a relationship has passed, we move into the "making it work" stage of the relationship. Sometimes the making it work stage is just not as much fun as the honeymoon stage. This is where the work part of making it work comes in.

One of the dangers of the making it work stage is to fall into what I call relationship ruts. A relationship rut is when as a couple you begin to feel as if you are stuck, sort of going through the motions and not getting anywhere. This is the point that some relationships die, because the only difference between a rut and a grave are the dimensions.

Let's take a look at some of the signs of relationship ruts and what not to do, and then what to do to get out of the rut and keep the spark alive.

121

♦ Signs of Relationship Ruts

One sure sign and conclusive evidence of a relationship rut is if the following conversation sounds familiar -

"What do want to do tonight?"
"I don't know, whatever you want to do."
"I don't know what I want to do, whatever you want to do is fine."
"Where do you want to eat?"
"I don't know, where do you want to eat?"
ETC - ETC - ETC - yuck!

Other signs of relationship ruts include:

- Doing the same thing over and over again and it not being enjoyable
- Having the same conversation over and over again
- Having that strange sense of "relationship deja vu" - we've been here before.
- arguing and bickering just for something to do
- What Not To Do

We all try to solve the problem of relationship ruts in our own way. Here are some solutions that I've seen couples try that are worth avoiding:

- keep doing the same things over and over and expect different results
- blame your partner or accuse them of being boring
- convince yourself that life would be much more fun with someone else
- make major changes just for the sake of change. For example, move (just a geographical cure) or have a child.
- What To Do

Having said all that, here are a few suggestions for breaking out of relationship ruts:

- Begin by remembering what is was that first attracted you to this person in the first place. You may have forgotten some things and may be surprised by what you remember.
- Do something "safely out of character." In the song "Dirt Gets Under The Fingernails" by Harry Chapin, the prim, proper and neat wife goes out and buys art supplies and makes a mess while the always dirty mechanic husband gets a shave, hair cut, manicure and new clothes. Surprise each other.
- Do some of the things you may have enjoyed as a child: buy a coloring book, some play dough, put on some roller skates, etc.
- Use your creativity! One way to do this would be to brainstorm all the crazy, absurd, and ridiculous ideas you can think of, that you would never do. Then go back over your list and see if there are the seeds for some useful creative solutions.
- Make a list of all the things you like to do for fun. Then pick one that you may not have done in a very long time.

As the songwriter says, making love stay can be one of the more difficult tasks in relationships. Avoiding and/or getting out of relationships ruts can go a long way to keeping the spark alive.

ACTION QUESTIONS

1) What ruts are you currently in in your relationship?
2) What will be the first steps you take to get out?

Marriage: Room Mates or Soul Mates?

*"Many marriages go from soul mates to room mates.
Only the most special make it back again."*

Jef Herring

Q: "My wife and I have been married for eight years now. Although there is nothing really wrong , we both feel the beginnings of boredom. It's almost like we are roommates instead of married. What's wrong?"

A: I believe you have asked a very good question. In fact, many people have written in recently to ask a very similar question. In the 20 years that I have been doing marriage therapy, I've been struck by the number of couples who seem to feel this way. It's almost as if, over time, they have moved from feeling like soul mates to merely roommates.

♦ From soul mate to roommate

In my ongoing work with couples, certain themes have come out that can help us in understanding how a couple that was once close can drift so far apart. Let's take a look at a few of these themes.

- Life got in the way. Somehow, in the midst of the hustle and bustle of everyday life, couples seem to almost forget about each other. The initial closeness they once felt has been damaged by focus on work, the bills, the kids, you name it.

- Taking each other for granted. A close cousin to the first reason, taking each other for granted slowly eats away at any connection a couple might feel. What makes it worse is that it is so very easy to do. Keeping priorities straight in our stressful lives can be very difficult. What I believe happens is we get so caught up in simply making a living that we forget about making a life with our partner.

- Stop treating each other well. Somehow we succumb to the notion that all the things we used to do that brought us together are no longer necessary. It's like the old joke about the couple who had been married for several years and one day the wife said to the husband, "You never say you love me anymore!" To which the husband replies, "Well, dear, I told you I loved you on our wedding day and if anything changes, I'll let you know."

- Holding resentments. Old grudges, hurts and resentments are like a cancer that eats away at the closeness of a couple.

- Stop communicating. This is the most frequent reason given by couples as a factor in their drifting apart. Once a couple stops communicating, it's just a matter of time before the roommate syndrome sets in.

♦ From roommate to soulmate

If you recognize your relationship in the above examples, hang in there, you are not alone and there is a way out. Couples don't plan on growing apart, they simply drift apart over time. Just the opposite is true about growing closer again. You don't just drift into it, you intentionally take action designed to grow closer together. Here are some tips from the couples I've worked with that have helped them to grow closer again.

- Remember when......? Have a conversation about how you first met and what first attracted you to each other.

- Similar to the first suggestion, talk about the times you have felt the most connection. Then list the things you did that helped create that closeness. Then do them again.

- This one comes from a reader who wrote in response to my question about what makes a successful marriage. She wrote in to say that while they will frequently say "I love you", like many other couples, it can become sort of cliche after awhile. What this couple does at the end of each day is to share something they each did that the other enjoyed. For example, "I loved it today when you gave me a break from the kids, or held my hand or hugged me, or helped me at the office, etc." Works for them, sounds good to me.

- Discover what your partner's "love language" is. Do they most need to see it, hear it, or feel it, in order to feel most loved. If you don't know , ask.
- Ask your partner what their "perfect day" would look like and then create as much of it as you can.
- Renew and/or rewrite your vows. Who says we can say these important words only once?! Renewing vows, commitments and words of love can rapidly and powerfully bring a couple closer together.

These are just a few suggestions for the road back to closeness and connection. I would love to hear from couples about how they have made the journey back to closeness after drifting apart. If you would like to share your secrets, just drop me a line.

ACTION QUESTIONS

1) What have you done to contribute to soul mate to room mate?

2) What do you need to do to go back to soul mates?

3 Key Ingredients for Marriage

"If you could design your relationship anyway
you wanted it, how would it be?"

Jef Herring

When people come in for marriage counseling, they typically come with a variety of expectations. Some people come expecting the therapist to tell one spouse they are wrong and the other right. Others come expecting to only talk about the problems in the marriage. Many come not knowing if they want to stay together or if they want to divorce. They just know they don't want it to continue as it has been.

Playing off of that last expectation, one of the questions I usually ask is "If you could design your relationship any way you wanted it, what would it be like?" Some common themes usually emerge, such as a sense of connection, feelings of closeness and friendship, and/or a desire for the passion they once felt for each other.

One of the more common themes I have noticed in recent years is summed up in the words "safety, intimacy, and fun." (Now there may be some clients out there right now saying, 'Look honey, he's writing about us!' Wrong. I write about ideas, not people. It's just that you folks give me so many good ideas.)

Safety, intimacy and fun. Each of these ingredients bring a special and important quality to marriage. Let's take a closer look at each of these important ingredients.

♦ Safety

While it's a given, it's important to say that safety from any kind of abuse is necessary for a marriage to thrive. If there is any kind of abuse occurring, get help immediately.

Having said that, there are a few other key ingredients that promote the sense of safety:

- freedom to express emotions. Being able to talk about how you feel without being told you are wrong for feeling that way is crucial in creating an atmosphere of safety.
- hearing the other person's emotions without making it a statement of your worth. Many couples get stuck on this one. Sometimes feelings just are. They are not necessarily a comment on the other person.
- a growing sense of trust. Sometimes in marriage trust can be damaged. It's important to make sure the trust level is increasing instead of decreasing.

♦ Intimacy

Often times when we talk about intimacy, we think of sex. While sex is an important (and fun) part of intimacy in marriage, they are many other factors that create intimacy.

Have you ever considered that intimacy is a skill? It's just not one we are often taught growing up, certainly not in school. Maybe they have Intimacy 101 now.

Here are a few of the key skills involved in intimacy:

- self-disclosure. The ability to talk about how you feel, and let some one in to your emotional world. In a sense, this is honoring the other person by saying you are important enough for me to share with you my deepest thoughts and feelings.
- vulnerability. Somehow we get the notion that we have to be tough and strong all the time. In a healthy relationship there is a trading back and forth of strength and vulnerability. It's a sign of trust in the relationship.
- empathy. The ability to step into the other's emotional world and "see through their eyes and feel through their heart."

♦ Fun

Many couples complain that they no longer have fun together. They feel like roommates at best and strangers at worst.

Part of the glue that holds marriages together is sharing fun times together. The memories of fun together can keep you going in the rough times as well.

Here are two suggestion for increasing the level of fun in your marriage:

- Think back to some of the most fun times you have had as a couple. Choose some of the things you did in the past. Now do them again. I know that sounds so simple, but it really can be. I guess I could make it harder for you, but why?

- Each partner make a list of things they like to do for fun. Exchange lists. Then each person gets to pick two things to do off of the other persons list. Plan on when to do them. Then do them.

Increasing the level of safety, intimacy and fun strengthens your marriage. You might want to try working on each of these areas over the next few months. Enjoy the changes, and keep the change.

ACTION QUESTIONS

1) What can you do to make your marriage a safe place?
2) What can you do to make your marriage an intimate place?
3) What can you do to make your marriage a fun place?

What Husbands & Wives Have to Say About Each Other

"Marriage is both the hardest thing I ever did and the smartest thing I ever did."

We have heard a lot lately about how different men and women are in relationships. Men are from this planet and women are from this other planet, etc. etc. And it's true. If you believe that men and women are different, congratulations, you just passed Anatomy 101. The differences go much deeper than physical characteristics, however. We can be as different emotionally as we are physically.

Now don't misunderstand me. I'm not saying one is better or worse, just different. Equality doesn't necessarily imply sameness.

One of the things I do in counseling and seminars with couples is to help them understand and appreciate the differences. One way I do this is by asking them to complete the following statements - "The hardest thing about being married/ a husband/ a wife is..."
"The best thing about being married/ a husband/ a wife is....."
"Something I wish my husband/wife understood about me is ......" "Something I wish I understood about my husband/wife is........"

Here are some excerpts from the insights of real live couples as they struggle to understand each other.
"The hardest thing about being married is........"
☞ Learning how to compromise and sometimes giving in to the other person.
☞ Realizing that my way is not always the right way or the only way to do something.
☞ Living with a morning person!

☞ I can't think of anything hard
☞ Husbands who leave the toilet seat up at night.
☞ Learning how to meet my partners emotional needs
☞ Disagreeing on how to handle the kids
☞ Communication - being open and vulnerable
☞ Keeping the spark in the relationship
☞ Avoiding getting in ruts after several years of marriage
☞ Being around someone all the time

"The best thing about being married is....................."
☞ having someone to share difficulties and good times with
☞ security of being with one person now & years to come
☞ companionship
☞ knowing that someone loves me and cares about me
☞ good sex
☞ shared responsibility
☞ sharing feelings and thoughts
☞ the comfort of being with someone
☞ hanging in there and making it work

"The hardest thing about being a husband is......"
☞ assuming responsibility for more than one person
☞ living with someone who is so different from you
☞ being a husband and a father
☞ handling emotion so much differently than my wife
☞ learning how to be sensitive to her feelings

"The best thing about being a husband is ...."
☞ not being alone
☞ the companionship of having someone to share life with
☞ having someone there to help me

"Something I wish my wife understood about me is ...."
☞ we sometimes do things or act inappropriately but it does not mean we love them less
☞ my need to be alone has nothing to do with her
☞ she is always on my mind, even when I am away
☞ my need to watch football

"Something I wish I understood about my wife is ...."
- ☞ their need to be shown love and attention constantly
- ☞ how long it takes to get over hurt feelings
- ☞ how to make her happy and meet her needs

"The hardest thing about being a wife is......"
- ☞ knowing what my husband's needs are
- ☞ trying to meet his needs
- ☞ dealing with a man's stubbornness

"The best thing about being a wife is ...."
- ☞ my husband looks to me as a source of comfort and advice
- ☞ feeling like I'm the most important person in his life
- ☞ "belonging" to someone
- ☞ having a place in a family
- ☞ my husband shares his life with me

"Something I wish my husband understood about me is ...."
- ☞ my husband is pretty understanding if I just let him know my feelings
- ☞ the little things that tend to make or break a relationship
- ☞ sometimes a woman just wants a hug or a kiss - not always leading to sex
- ☞ sometimes I just need to be held
- ☞ sometimes I just want him to listen to me without having to "fix" anything - JUST LISTEN

"Something I wish I understood about my husband is ...."
- ☞ why he places so much value on material things and career
- ☞ their deep emotional feelings
- ☞ why he doesn't talk about problems and concerns in order to resolve them
- ☞ why they don't stop & ask for directions when they are lost

Pay attention to the common themes to see what can be learned and used in your own relationship.

If you have any views that you would like to add, please let me know, and they may be included in future columns.

ACTION QUESTIONS

1) What's the best thing for you about marriage?
2) What's the hardest thing for you about marriage?
3) What's something you wish you understood about your spouse?
4) What's something you wish your spouse understood about you?
5) Now go share these answers with your spouse.

The Gentle Arts of Apology & Forgiveness

"I'm sor-, I'm so-, I'm sorr-"
Fonzie in Happy Days

Remember the 1970 movie "Love Story" starring Ryan O'Neal and Ali McGraw? The popular saying from the movie became "Love means never having to say you're sorry." By the end of the movie, the character played by Ali McGraw dies of cancer, so we don't get to see the long term results of believing that love means never having to say you're sorry. My guess is they would have either had to re-think that idea or the relationship would have died of the cancer of wounded feelings and resentment.

In my experience, *being able* to say you are sorry is one of the key ingredients to a lasting relationship, especially in marriage.

Any long term relationship of any depth will have conflict. I would even go so far as to agree with noted communications author Paul Waltslavick who wrote, "With out conflict, there is no relationship." I would add that without the healthy resolution of conflict, there is no lasting healthy relationship.

Two of the many skills necessary for a lasting relationship are the ability to apologize and the ability to forgive. Let's take a closer look at each of these skills.

Any one can say the words "I'm sorry." That's the easy part. For an apology to be genuine however, more needs to be done. I learned this lesson the hard way through a small incident in grad school. I lived next door to a Suwanee Swifty convenience store and stopped in one day for a soda and candy bar (the staples of grad students). When I reached into the cooler for the coke I knocked one off the shelf and it burst open on the floor of the back room. I casually offered an "I'm sorry" to the regular and usually friendly clerk, who seemed angry that day. The next time I was in we got to talking about what had happened. What he said to me was so true, "Anybody can say I'm sorry. I could punch you in the face and say I'm sorry, but your face would still be hurt."

What I learned from this is that in order to be truly sorry, at least one, if not all of these three things need to happen:

- Amends need to be made. In the shattered coke story I needed to have cleaned up the mess or paid for it, or both.
- Asking for forgiveness.
- A commitment to a change in behavior needs to be made.

Saying I'm sorry can be easy. Making amends can be time consuming and inconvenient. Asking for forgiveness is truly humbling and the difficult part, especially in marriage. Without forgiveness in marriage, anger, resentment and frustration become like hardening cement. As a result, people stay stuck in those feelings and begin to view all future interactions through those feelings.

Forgiving someone can be equally, if not more difficult. Part of what can make forgiving so difficult in relationships has to do with several myths about forgiveness.

- Myth 1 - In order to forgive, I have to feel like it. Waiting until you feel like forgiving someone could leave you waiting for a very long time. Forgiveness, much like genuine love, is a decision, an act of the will, not a just a feeling
- Myth 2 - If I forgive, I let them off the hook and leave my self vulnerable for it to happen again. Forgiveness is not for the other person's benefit, it's for yours. A wise friend once told me that not forgiving someone is much like trying to crush a sandspur between your fingers. You might eventually do it, but it's sure going to hurt you.
- Myth 3 - Forgiving someone condones what they did. Quite the contrary, forgiving someone simply releases you

from the pain and hurt of their actions.. It might also help you to stop seeing your self as a victim.

Having said all that, here are some questions for you to consider about apologies and forgiveness in your own life.

- To whom and what for might you need to apologize?
- What kind of amends might you need to make?
- Whose forgiveness do you need to ask?
- Who do you need to forgive? Someone else or perhaps yourself?
- What might it cost you to do these things?
- What might it cost you not to do these things?

Here's one more thing to consider before I let you go. How would your relationship be different if you and your partner said the following to each other every day for a week:

- "I apologize for............"
- "Please forgive me for.........."
- "I forgive you for.........."

ACTION QUESTIONS

1) What gets in the way of apologizing?
2) What gets in the way of forgiving?
3) For what do you need to apologize?
4) For what do you need to forgive?

Couples & Conflict

*"Why does it always seem to be
Me lookin' at you
You lookin' at me"*
Phil Collins

Conflict. Arguments. Fighting. Or as my parents used to call it "loud discussions." Whatever you call it, disagreements come to all relationships. And whether you have been married for just a few months or for many years, conflict in marriage is quite normal. In fact, Paul Watslavick, the noted communications expert, has gone as far as saying, "without conflict, there is no relationship." I would simply add that without the healthy resolution of conflict, it is unlikely that the relationship will last, much less thrive.

One of the problems is there can be so much in marriage for two people to come into conflict over. It can be one of what I call the big six - communication, children, money, sex, in-laws, and religion. Or the issue can be something as major as the proper washing and drying of dishes. Whatever the issue, it is the healthy resolution of conflict that can make or break a relationship.

The problem, at least in my experience, is a frustrating trait most humans seem to have. We all like to be right. And we tend to argue for our positions. Some more than others. Then we get to win at the expense of the relationship.

It's like the story of how a certain Indian tribe would settle severe conflicts among it's members. The two combatants were bound together at the wrist and then given the weapon of their choice for the other hand. They could then begin the battle. Whatever the outcome, the two were to remain bound together after the battle. Kind of sounds like marriage, doesn't it?

Here's the question I believe it all comes down to, "Do you want to be right or do you want to be happy?" In my experience with couples, sometimes the whole relationship can come down to the answer to that question.

Let's take a closer look at the characteristics of each of these two choices.

- ◆ Wanting to be right
- defending your position at all costs
- wearing the other person down
- taking the "my way or the highway" approach
- debating the logic of your position. Many partners have told me that often times they don't even believe what they are saying, they just want to win.
- making winning the argument more important than solving the conflict
- creating win-lose situations
- catching yourself sounding like one of your parents arguing. This can mean that some old and perhaps destructive patterns are beginning to emerge.
- making your needs more important than your partner's and/or the needs of the relationship. The approach of one person always getting their needs met, while the other person loses can work for awhile. It eventually falls apart as the resentment and distance grows.

Now let's take a look at some of the key phrases used by couples who want to be happy.

- ◆ Wanting to be happy
- "Let's try it your way." Sometimes difficult words to say. But consider this notion for a moment. You chose

this person, out of all the world, to be your life partner. What does it say about you that you don't even consider their view as valuable and important?

- "Maybe you're right." A close cousin to the first, it demonstrates that you are willing to consider another view than your own.
- "What do you think?" Invites the other person to share their view and draws them closer to you.
- "What's good for my spouse is good for me." I first heard this concept from a gentleman on a New Orleans radio interview I did on what makes a successful relationship. Now some people might say this is codependent or unhealthy in some other way. I remember the gentleman sounded fairly happy. I'd be willing to bet his wife is fairly happy as well.

These are just a few of the ways we can show that we want to be happy instead of right. I'm sure you can come up with others.

Giving up the need, or the "right to be right" does not mean giving in and being walked on. It does mean being strong enough to be vulnerable. It also means putting being happy above being right. It's not always an easy thing to do. However, the rewards seem to be worth the struggle.

ACTION QUESTIONS

1) Where are you caught in wanting to be right?
2) Where can you begin to change things in order to be happy?

Checkbook Battles - Couples & Money

"Money is green energy"

Tony Robbins

"You can't hold onto a dime. Do you own the mall yet?!" "It takes a crowbar to open your wallet. You can't take it with you, ya know!!" If these words or ones like them sound all too familiar, you may be experiencing "checkbook battles" in your relationship. Checkbook battles are simply couples fighting about the issue of money. In marriage, the "Big 6" areas of potential conflict are communication, sex, children, in-laws, religion and, you guessed it, MONEY! (Not to mention the proper way in which to wash and dry the dishes). For many couples, money can become a vicious battleground.

One of the most interesting things about helping couples deal with this issue is how uncomfortable people are talking about money. Almost any issue, even sex, seems to be more easily discussed than the issue of money. Many couples have never discussed it at all, except to argue about it. It's not surprising that research shows that a full 60% of divorces can be traced back to conflicts over money.

So why all the conflict over money? In my experience working with couples, I have discovered that people tend to look at money in some very different ways.

A useful definition of money is simply that it is "green energy." The way that we handle and relate to this green energy is called our "money style." Our money style is determined by at least two factors. The first is the emotional meaning we give to money. The second is the way money was handled in the family in which we grew up.

Where many couples get into difficulty is they have different emotional meanings for money. Consider, if you will, what the emotional meaning of money is for you. Is it security, power, pleasure, control, independence? Or perhaps something else? How is it the same and how is it different from your partner's?

Secondly, how was money handled in the family you grew up in? Were your parents savers or big spenders? If your partner is significantly different from you in this area, there is the potential for checkbook battles.

Consider, for example, one couple that came for counseling. Let's call them Bob and Mary for this story. See if you can pick up the differences in this couples money style.

In the family Bob grew up in, money was simply a means to an end. The end was fun and pleasure. If you wanted something, you bought it. It didn't matter if the numbers didn't add up. "Can't afford it" had little or no meaning.

The only savings this person knows about is the "investment" in their own fun and pleasure.

Mary, on the other hand, grew up quite differently. In her family, money meant security and self-esteem. In order to spend over a certain small amount, the purchase had to be thoroughly researched. At least three comparisons had to be made, with many resources, including Consumer Reports, having to be consulted.

After much deliberation, a decision was made, the money was spent, and then she felt guilty about it.

Can you pick out the different emotional meanings for these two people? Think there just might be some potential for conflict?

If you find that you and your partner have different money styles, don't be alarmed. Most folks do. The good news is there are many things that can be done to help blend the differing styles.

Here are a list of do's and don'ts that not only helped Bob and Mary avoid the checkbook battles, they strengthened their relationship as well.

- ♦ DON'T
- assume that your way is the only right way. Avoid the seven deadly words, "I've always done it that way before."
- accuse your partner of being sinful or wrong
- try to force your partner to see it your way
- handle it your way in secret, behind your partners back
- ♦ DO
- identify your own money style
- identify your partner's money style
- learn some flexibility. Five words that lead to solutions are "Let's try it your way."
- explore your goals for life together, remembering you are a team, not competitors
- try switching roles- let the bill payer do the shopping and the shopper do the bill paying
- discover what you might need to learn from your partner's style

One way to combine the two styles is to create a reasonable working budget. Two keys to making a budget work are:

- have an agreed upon amount of money that cannot be spent unless it is first discussed,
- each person has a small amount of money that they can use however they wish, no questions asked.

If you continue to remain stuck on this issue, it might be useful to consult a financial planner, a marriage counselor, or both.

Remember that the goal is to blend your styles together so that instead of causing conflict, this "green energy" called money works for you and grows you closer together. Come to think of it, blending styles together and growing closer seems like a good goal for any issue.

ACTION QUESTIONS

1) Growing up, how was money handled in your family?
2) How is it different from and similar to your spouse's?
3) What is your money style?
4) What can you do to begin to blend your two styles together?

Building Trust

"It's always been a matter of trust"

Billy Joel

Q: "I read your column each week and have found it to be a wonderful source of information on relationships. I am writing to ask you to please devote a future column on trust, or more specifically, how to trust again in a new relationship."

A: Thanks for reading and for your kind words. I'll do my best to answer your question about what is really a fairly complex and misunderstood issue.

Billy Joel once sang "It's always been a matter of trust." While that may be true, trust can be a complex issue because there are so many pieces that go into having trust for a person.

In an attempt to simplify the issue of trust, I've broken it down into five components, one for each letter of the word trust. TRUST stand for inTegrity, Responsibility, Understanding, Security and Time. Let's look at each one these components more closely.

♦ inTegrity - Funk and Wagnalls defines integrity as "uprightness of character." Sounds nice, but what does that really mean? To put hands and feet on the issue, a person has integrity when their behavior matches their words. They do what they say they are going to do. If, over time, their behavior consistently does not match their words, watch out.

♦ Responsibility - People mess up and make mistakes. That's just a part of every day life. People that can be trusted take responsibility for their mistakes. They don't blame others or make excuses. When they mess up, they admit it and do what is necessary to fix it if at all possible.

144

♦ Understanding - Another sign of trustworthiness is the ability to understand another person. Especially in a close relationship such as marriage, you may not always agree with the other person. You may not always see things the exact same way. However, in order for trust to grow, you need to be able to see the world through their eyes, which is another definition of understanding.

♦ Security - We tend to trust the people with whom we feel secure. In this context, secure means safe. We feel like we can be ourselves around them and say what we really think and feel.

♦ Time - Time is a crucial factor when it comes to building trust. All of the above components, integrity, responsibility, understanding and security, are all developed and demonstrated over time. Especially for people who have been hurt before, it takes time to develop trust in someone.

Time is also a contributing factor in some of the confusion about trust. We tend to think of trust as an either/or proposition. Either you have 100% trust or none at all. In reality, trust is a much more manageable issue if you think of it in terms you can measure.

When we are dealing with a loosely defined concept such as trust, sometimes it can be useful to quantify it. To quantify something means to create a way to measure something that is in reality unmeasurable.

In order to quantify trust, let's put it on a scale of 1 to 10, with one being the least amount of trust and 10 being the most. The nice thing about a scale from one to ten is that it gives us a lot of room between one and ten, and not just the either/or absolutes.

Now, here's a useful little exercise about trust. This is especially useful if you are in a relationship where trust has been damaged and both people want to build the trust back.

Using our 1 to 10 scale, rate the level of trust in four different ways. Give a number to 1) where it is now, 2) the worst it's ever been, 3) the best it's ever been, and 4) how you would like it to be. You should now have four numbers. Like many people, you may notice that where it is now is higher than the worst it's ever been. If that is so, what did it take to move up the scale? The answers to that question are part of what helps you to build trust in a person.

Now let's do a little higher math. Take the number from where it is now and subtract it from the number of where you would like it to be. For sake of example, let's say it's 10 minus 5, which is 5. That means you have five levels of trust to go to get where you want. Instead of trying to jump from five to ten in one shot, let's break it down into more manageable chunks. What small, day to day things would it take to go from a 5 to a 6? Then from a 6 to a 7? A 7 to an 8, and so on.

In this way, a person can build trust back over time. It also allows you to see if the person's behavior matches their words, which is one of the main signs of trust.

Thanks again for an excellent question, and I hope this answer has been helpful to you. I wish you happy trust building!

ACTION QUESTIONS

1) How do you rate on each of the pillars of trust?
2) If you haven't already done so, do the exercise on trust. Go ahead, do it now.

For Your Own Sake, Learn to Forgive

"Not forgiving someone is like trying to crush a sandspur between your fingers. You might eventually do it, but it's sure gonna hurt."

Joe Mills

A recent episode of NBC's ER got me thinking about the concept of forgiveness in relationships, especially marriage. One of the subplots in the Thursday night drama is about a staff member that is HIV positive, infected by her ex-husband who got the disease while having one of several affairs.

In the recent episode, she treated a woman who had attempted suicide and was dying. It turns out that the patient had contracted the HIV virus while having an affair, and not only gave it to her husband but her unborn child as well. The child later died. When the woman's husband was summoned to the hospital, he told the nurse, with a great deal of bitterness, "I've been waiting for this day. I wouldn't miss it."

Later in the show, while the nurse was talking with her ex-husband, he asks her, "Can you forgive me?" Her response, "I already have. I got tired of the anger. I decided I didn't want to be that kind of person."

While that was certainly quite a lot to forgive, it does speak to the need for and the power of forgiveness in our lives.

While forgiveness may sound like one of those "touchy-feely", self-help movement issues, it's really not. In fact, there is an increasing body of scientific research into the concept of forgiveness. The January issue of The Journal of Marital and Family Therapy states that "forgiveness is reported to be an effective intervention regarding problems" in issues from anger and depression to broken marital relationships (Hargrave and Sells, 1997).

147

If we haven't already, all of us will face the task of forgiving hurts in our lives at some point. When confronted with the choice to forgive in relationships, we can either get bitter or get better. Let's look at how to get bitter, some barriers to forgiveness, and finally, how to get better.

♦ How to Get Bitter
- Remind the person, often, of the offense
- Replay the situation over and over in your mind
- Get friends and family on your side
- Nurse the hurt. Better yet, pick at it, like a sore on the body.
- Give the other person no chance to change.
- Listen *only* to the history. What does that mean? Many times, history whispers with a very loud voice. It goes something like, "Don't you dare forgive that, you know it will just happen again. It always does," or "There he/she goes again, just like all the times before."

"But aren't we supposed to learn from our experience?" you might be saying at this point. Of course we are. While it's true that "those that forget the past are condemned to repeat it," if you focus only on the past, you can often get the same result.

♦ Barriers to Forgiveness
Most barriers to forgiveness come in the form of a "but." For example -
- "But I don't feel like forgiving." And you may not for a while. Ultimately, forgiveness is a decision, not a feeling.
- "But if I forgive someone, doesn't that mean I approve of what they did?" No, not at all. Forgiveness does not condone what was done.
- "But if I forgive, doesn't that open me up to be hurt again?" Well, yes and no. The yes part is that if we are going to risk closeness in relationships, we are going to

148

risk being hurt. It's just part of the territory. The no part is that while forgiving, you can still protect yourself from further hurt. One way to do this is in relationships is to set clear boundaries with equally clear consequences if the boundaries are violated.

- "But if I forgive, doesn't that let the other person off the hook?" Not necessarily. There are consequences for actions, even after forgiveness. What forgiveness can do is let you off the hook of bitterness and resentment.
- "But I forgave, and I still feel bad." Unfortunately, that can happen. While it's true that forgiveness is a decision, it's also a process. So is the healing. It can take time.

♦ How to Get Better

Forgiveness is not easy. It is worth it. Here are some tips on how to forgive and move from "bitterness to betterness."

The first two tips involve decisions:

- Decision #1 - Do I want to "blame and be-lame?" When we get caught in blame, it cripples us and makes us lame.
- Decision #2 - Is the relationship more important than the injury? Deciding that the relationship is more important than the injury opens the door to forgiveness. It's like poet Hugh Prather said, "Friends eventually forgive and come back together because we need friends more than we need pride."
- Sometimes you just have to tell history to shut up!
- Ultimately, forgiveness is not for the other person, it's for yourself. Why? Two reasons:
- Forgiveness can release you from the pain of bitterness and resentment
- Forgiveness allows you to move on with your life and relationships.

Again, I realize that what I am suggesting here is by no means easy. It can sometimes be one of the most difficult things we ever do. By the same token, it can also be one of the most worthwhile. It comes down to a choice, bitter or better. What will it be for you?

ACTION QUESTIONS

1) In how many ways are you working on "getting bitter?"
2) In how many ways are you working on "getting better?"

The 3 C's of Resolving Conflict

"And they lived happily ever after..........."

Old fairy tale

We seem so unprepared for how to handle conflict. We know in our heads that "happily ever after" is true only in stories and fairly tales, yet in our hearts we long for it to be true.

In the best of all possible worlds, we would be well prepared for handling conflict before we get married. My experience in my office tells me that is just not the case for most couples.

Part of the reason for this is there is just so much in a marriage relationship that can cause conflict. I've written before about what's called the Big Six, the six main areas of conflict in marriage. The Big Six are the areas of communication, money, sex, children, in-laws and religion. Perhaps we should call it the Big Seven, and add the all important issue of who gets to hold the TV remote control . No kidding, I've actually had couples fighting over this issue. I've even had them fighting over the age old issue of how to hang the toilet paper roll, over or under. When I suggested that when you consider what you will use the toilet paper for, it really doesn't matter, it seemed to clear up the issue.

Humor goes a long way in resolving conflict.

Having said all that, let's look at some specific ways to handle conflict in marriage. This is called the three C's of conflict resolution and they stand for Compromise, Co-exist and Capitulation. Let's take a closer look at each of these methods.

151

♦ Compromise

"A compromise would surely help the situation."

10CC

Compromise is clearly the optimal solution to conflict. The problem comes when couples approach conflict as a win-lose situation, which makes it very difficult to reach a compromise. It's simply human nature to want to be right, and so we approach resolving conflict from a right or wrong perspective.

What this typically leads to is one person usually getting their way or their needs met at the expense of the other person. While this may work for awhile, it eventually leads to bitterness and resentment.

Compromise, on the other hand, becomes a win-win situation. A couple approaches conflict resolution from a team mate/partner perspective. There are basically three key ingredients to compromise:

- each person gives a little
- each person gets as many needs met as possible
- each person works for the good of the relationship, not their own desires.

♦ Capitulation

"Let's try it your way."

An experienced and wise spouse

I can hear it now. "But isn't capitulation just giving in and being codependent with someone?" It can be, if done on a regular basis over time. Over the course of a marriage, or any long term relationship, for that matter, there are times when the best thing to do is try it the other persons way. The capitulating partner comes from a place that basically says, "Our relationship and our happiness is more important to me than this issue. Let's try it your way."

That's not codependency, it's cooperation.

♦ Co-exist

"There's only you and me and we just disagree."

Dave Mason

There are times in marriage where each spouse feels strongly enough about their beliefs or position that they can not move or come to the other person's side. There are certainly some issues in marriage where this could signal the end of the relationship. However, in most circumstances, couples can simply agree to disagree, and move on. They learn to "co-exist" on the issue in question.

I know of many couples who have taken this route on various issues and continue to have very strong marriages. What can happen over time, after being given the room to each have their opinion, spouses are able to move into compromise. Even if couples remain in a co-existing position on an issue, they can still have a strong marriage.

Conflict in marriage is inevitable. The successful handling of conflict involves a healthy and balanced mix of the skills of compromise, capitulation and co-existing. No matter how you hang the toilet paper.

ACTION QUESTIONS

1) How can you apply the skill of compromise to your marriage?

2) How can you apply the skill of capitulation to your marriage?

3) How can you apply the skill of co-existing to your marriage?

Valentine's Day Gifts from the Heart

"But I thought you needed a blender"
A well-meaning and confused husband

With Valentine's Day right around the corner, a reader recently wrote to ask, *"With Valentine's Day coming up, do you have any suggestions for how I can show love to my spouse that would be different from the same old flowers and candy kind of thing? Even though I feel like those gifts are still expected, I'd like to find something new and creative, but on a tight budget. Maybe something that's not a material thing. What would you suggest?"*

What a great and challenging question! I took the challenge and have been asking clients, friends, colleagues and my wife for creative, romantic and inexpensive suggestions. As a result of this extensive scientific research, here are one marriage counselor's suggestions for Valentine's Day gifts.

• Ask your partner what a perfect day might look like for them. And then to whatever extent possible, create that day for them.

• Create a scrapbook or collage of your first date. Include pictures, ticket stubs, and memories of that time together.

• Talk about the times the two of you were the closest. Then pick two or three things from that time that you can intentionally do again.

• Find out some of the dreams of your partner. How? Just ask. These can be things from childhood or from the present time, small scale and large scale. Then see how many you can fulfill. In our house, we have a make believe company called "Dreams Come True, Inc." From time to time, one of us will give the other a card with the Dreams Come True logo, along with the dream, or some part of it, that goes with it. It's a kick and it really shows you have been listening.

- Write a love note to you partner. If you have trouble coming up with what to say, here are a few suggestions -
- write about what first attracted you to your partner and what still attracts you now
- apologize for something from the past
- appreciate something in the present
- anticipate something in the future
- if you like to travel, here's a suggestion from my wife. Find out about a place your partner would love to go that you may not be able to afford yet. Let's say Italy for example. Then here's what you do - go to the video store and rent travel movies about and/or movies set in Italy. Get brochures and maps from AAA or a travel agency. Cook Italian, and make it Italian night in your house. Not too hard to guess what I'll be doing for Valentine's Day, huh?
- Ask your partner a rather simple, yet profound question; "What does love look like to you." You may be very surprised to find out that it is different from what love may look like to you. What you now have is the beginning of a map to guide you in expressing love toward your partner.
- If you are currently doing anything in the relationship that is not working, remember the first rule of ruts - when you are in one, stop digging. Find something, almost anything, to do differently to get out of the rut.
- for one week, take over a household task that you know your partner dislikes
- Here's one called the treasure hunt gift. Whatever gift you get your partner, make a game out of finding it. Leave a card with a note suggesting they look somewhere for the next clue. Then in that place leave another note about where to find the next clue, and the next one, etc., leading up to the place where you have hidden the gift. I'll leave the rest to your own imagination.

•   If you have access to the equipment, record a cassette tape of music. Include favorite songs the two of you have, as well as songs that express how you feel about your partner.

•   If at all possible, take a day off or use a weekend day and just go play. Play games, go to a park and swing, fly kites, blow bubbles - whatever you remember as fun from childhood. It can be really romantic, as well as a great stress reliever.

My thanks to all those who offered suggestions for romantic and simple gifts. I hope these suggestion will be useful to you. If you really wanted to go all out, you could do all of them together. The twelve days of Valentine's Day, perhaps. And don't forget the flowers and candy. Happy Valentine's Day!

P.S. These things could be done any day of the year.

ACTION QUESTIONS

1) Which of these would most surprise your spouse?
2) Can you add any to the list?

The Universal Laws of Marriage

"Gravity doesn't care if you believe in it or not"

In the theme song for the hit TV sitcom "Mad About You", they call marriage "the final frontier."

They sure got that one right. In my experience helping people to get the changes they want in their lives, it's been my observation that the marriage relationship is one of the most challenging.

In light of that observation, today's column offers a few "universal laws" for a successful marriage. A universal law in the physical world is something like gravity. It doesn't matter if you ignore it, don't believe in it, or don't think it applies to you. If you violate the law of gravity by jumping off a high building and haven't arranged for a gentle glide or a soft landing, you will go splat. In the same way, violate any of these universal laws of marriage once too often, and you might go splat as a couple.

♦ The Law of Three People

When you marry someone, you don't marry one person, you marry three. The person you think they are, the person they really are, *and the person they are going to become as a result of marrying you.*

♦ The Law of Competition

Competition between spouses in a marriage is like cancer in the body. If left untreated, it eventually kills the marriage.

♦ The Law of Nagging

I've never seen a situation where one person was being accused of nagging where the other person was not being irresponsible in some way.

157

♦ The Law of Emotional Needs

Most, if not all, conflict in marriage can be traced to unmet needs. What are your spouses' emotional needs? If you find your self in the middle of a conflict, what emotional needs have not been met?

♦ Law of Fun

The couple that laughs and plays together, has a much better chance of staying together.

♦ The Law of Communication, Part 1

Human communications expert Paul Waltzslavick once said, " You cannot not communicate." If this is true, the question then becomes "what am I communicating, on a regular basis, to my spouse?"

♦ The Law of Communication, Part 2

It's the responsibility of the person talking to make sure that the message is getting across.

♦ The Law of Communication, Part 3

At the same time, it's the responsibility of the person listening to make sure they got what the other person was saying.

♦ The Law of Politeness

In most marriages, it's all to easy to begin taking each other for granted. It's important to continue to treat each other well. When you need to get by someone, saying "excuse me" is still a whole let better than "move."

♦ The Law of Underwear

Related to the law of politeness, it comes under the heading of taking each other for granted. So don't hang around in your underwear, unless it's sexy.

♦ The Law of Connection

Spouses are either growing closer or growing apart. You don't get to stand still in relationships. So we need to know two things, 1) what does it take to continue to feel connected to my spouse?, and 2) what does it take for my spouse to continue to feel connected to me?

♦ The Law of "The Other Person's Eyes"

In marriage, we don't have to always agree with our partner, of even see things the exact same way. We do need to be able to step into the other person's world and be able to see through their eyes.

So there we are, some universal laws for marriage. I'm sure you can offer additional, perhaps better ones from your own experience. We'd love to hear from you and perhaps feature them in a future column.

Thanks for reading, and keep the change!

ACTION QUESTIONS

1) What universal laws have you consistently violated in your marriage?
2) What would happen if you stopped?
3) What universal laws can you add from your own marriage?

Honor in Relationships

"To honor someone means to put them first"

Jef Herring

Recently in a seminar on marriage I was asked a very disturbing question. It went something like this, "Don't you think the phrase 'love, honor and cherish' in the wedding vows is a little outdated for the 90's." My answer was "Absolutely, positively not!!" I went on to say that the application of the promise to love, honor and cherish was needed now more than ever in relationships.

Remember your wedding vows? Most of us were just too nervous to really know or think about what "love, honor and cherish" really meant.

I've always been fascinated by the word honor. Exactly what does it mean to honor our partner? Webster defines honor in this way, "the center point of the upper half of an armorial escutcheon." Not very useful for our purposes, huh? Webster also defines honor as "to hold in high regard or esteem." Now that's more like it!

While working with couples, I often ask them this question, "How do you honor each other?" Many times I often receive just blank looks in return.

Isn't it interesting that most of us said those words without really knowing what they mean?

So let's figure it out. Often times one of the best ways to learn how to do something is to learn how not to do it as well. Let's take a look at some ways to dishonor our partners, and then look at some key ways to honor our partners.

♦ How to dishonor
• Ignore them. Put everything else in life before them.

- Exhaust yourself at work. Leave your partner just the crumbs of your attention.
- Criticize them to your friends. While wife- and husband-bashing may be a popular past time, it can easily create distance in a relationship.
- Criticize their opinions.
- Be a "Darren Stevens." Huh, you say? Remember the TV sitcom Bewitched, that we can still catch on Nick at Night? Darren didn't want Samantha to use her magical powers, so he blocked her whenever he could. I always thought that was pretty dumb, since he could have had anything he wanted. Being a "Darren Stevens" means blocking your partner from using their natural gifts and reaching their potential.
- not giving your full attention to your partner
- How to honor
- Place them high on your priority list
- Ask their opinion. Remember, they chose to be with you. Hopefully that means they make good choices and have valuable opinions.
- Spend time with them. The gift of time is one of the most precious we can share. Doing things together is a wonderful way to spend time together. Remember that it's also important to spend the kind of time where your partner has your full attention, and you are completely focused on each other.
- Brag about them to your friends.
- I know many couples who keep their partner's shoe size, dress size or favorite color on a piece of paper in their wallet or purse. What would it be like if we added to that list such things as dreams and wishes, desires of the heart, favorite ways to be treated, etc?

In closing, here are two questions to consider:

- What would it feel like to be honored by your partner on a day to day basis?
- And perhaps more importantly, what would happen if you honored your partner on a day to day basis?

ACTION QUESTIONS

1) This is a tough one - in how many ways have you dishonored your partner in the past?

2) In how many ways do you continue to dishonor your partner?

3) In how many ways can you commit to honoring your partner, now and in the future?

How to Turn Love into Action

"How do we make love stay?"

Dan Fogleberg

Q: A reader writes to ask, "We have been married for ten years now and things are good. We still love each other and believe we have a strong marriage. What can we do to make it even better and stronger?"

A: What a nice and rarely asked question! I think it's great to want to strengthen and improve an already healthy marriage.

One of the problems is we are taught some interesting, confusing, and sometimes misleading notions about love and marriage in our society. Take for example the following quotes from movies and music -

- "Love means never having to say your sorry" - Love Story
- "Love will keep us together" - The Captain and Tenille
- "Love hurts" - Nazareth
- "Love conquers all" - Seals and Crofts
- "All we need is love" - The Beatles

It seems the popular notion is that if we have the feeling of love for someone, the rest is just details and smooth sailing. In my experience of working with couples in both counseling and workshops, having the feeling of love is only the beginning point. After that, successful relationships require taking action based on that love. I call this "putting hands and feet" on the feeling of love.

In the book Chicken Soup for the Soul by Jack Canfield and Mark Victor Hansen (Health Communications, $12.00), a book I highly recommend, the authors begin their section on love with the following quote from Tielhard de Chardin, "The day will come when, after harnessing space, the winds, the tides and gravitation, we shall harness for God the energies of

163

love. And on that day, for the second time in the history of the world, we shall have discovered fire."

A powerful quote that seems to capture the power of putting hands and feet on the feeling of love. The big question, at least in terms of marriage relationships, is how do we take action and demonstrate that love on a daily basis?

Authors, therapists and married couple Bill O'Hanlon and Pat Hudson give us some guidance in their book, aptly titled, Love is a Verb (W.W. Norton and Co., $19.95). The subtitle of their book is "How to stop analyzing your relationship and start making it great." In other words, while there is a place for understanding the *why* of your relationship, the focus needs to be on the *how* of making it better, on solutions. The authors state, "Solution-oriented therapy focuses on people's strengths and inner resources, bypasses a lot of analysis, and gives people concrete ways of changing their actions and their points of view."

The main goal of strengthening a relationship is not to analyze/understand it better. The main goal is to be able to do things that improve and strengthen the relationship. Along those lines, here are some suggestions, from the O'Hanlons and myself, on how to put hands and feet onto love in your relationship -

- Make a list of "little things" you know your partner likes and enjoys. Keep it with you (in your wallet, briefcase, purse, bathroom mirror) to remind you.
- Discover your partners definition of love. How? Simple, ASK!
- Ask your partner, "what can I do today (this week, month, year, lifetime) that will help you feel loved by me?"
- Catch your partner doing something you appreciate, and then tell them.
- You and your partner fill in the blanks to this question, "I feel closest to you when............"

- Think back over the history of your relationship to something you did that brought the biggest smile to your partners face. If at all possible, DO IT AGAIN!!
- Ask your partner, "what would a perfect day look like to you?" And then create as much of that perfect day as you can.
- A very simple yet profound action is to consider together the times you have felt the closest. Make a list of the things you were doing that contributed to the feeling of closeness, and take the time to do them again. You may not be able to do every detail of the last three suggestions. That's alright, just do what parts you can.

Good, strong, lasting relationships don't just happen, they are actively created by putting hands and feet on love.

It's true, the Beatles did say "all we need is love." But remember, they broke up.

ACTION QUESTIONS

1) What suggestions from this column can you use right away?
2) Why are you still reading, why aren't you doing them?
Go do them now!

7 Seeds to Grow a Healthy Marriage

"God's great cosmic joke on the human race was to require that men and women live together in marriage."

Mark Twain

Q: We enjoy reading your weekly column and noticed that you give seminars too. I think that you mentioned a seminar for couples some time ago, and we were wondering what kind of seminar you do and how we can find out more. Is it just for couples that are having problems or is it for people like us that have a good marriage that we want to make better?

In my seminar for couples, ***The 7 Seeds for Growing a Healthy Marriage,*** we look at seven key factors that go into building a strong marriage. The seminar is specifically designed so that couples who are struggling to stay together as well as couples who simply want to make a good marriage better can all benefit.

So in today's column, I'll do two things:

♦ briefly describe each of the 7 seeds
♦ give you just one of the many key strategies for implementing each of the 7 seeds in your own marriage.

Commitment - True commitment means much more than simply committing to staying married. Here's one of my favorite quotes about marriage, "When you marry, you don't marry one person, you marry three. The person you think they are, they person they really are, *and the person they are going to become as a result of marrying you."*

Key strategy: Genuine commitment involves being committed to the growth and best interests of your partner. Or as one

166

wise married person said to me on a recent radio show, *"What's good for my partner is good for me."*

Teamwork - There was once a couple who went by the name of Mr. Neat and Ms. Clean. Mr. Neat could bath in a shower full of soap scum and not mind at all as long as the towels and soap were neat and in their place. Ms. Clean can have piles and piles of stuff scattered everywhere, as long as the piles are clean. This couple can have either a very neat and clean home or a real mess on their hands, depending on their ability to work together as a team.

Key strategy: Use the five most important words in marriage: "Let's try it your way."

Communication - Without exception, every couple that I have ever worked with struggle with effective communication. Part of the reason for this is that two people with the exact same communication style rarely marry each other. Because of this factor, we often times misunderstand what the other person is saying and then react to what we think we have heard.

Key strategy: Use the ten most important words in marriage: "Let me see if I get what you are saying."

Meeting emotional needs - In the same way that two people with the same communication style rarely marry each other, couples rarely have the same emotional needs. What happens is that each of us give what we would most like to get, but the other person may not want that at all.

Key strategy - Discover and then meet the emotional needs of your partner. How? Simple. *Ask!*

Resolving conflict - Conflict in marriage is inevitable. Fighting is optional. For some folks that's a revolutionary idea. The bottom line is that many times in marriage you have a choice: you can be right or you can be happy, but you can't be both.

Key strategy: Stay away from "my way" or "your way" battles. Focus on "our way" solutions, or as Stephen Covey says "win-win" solutions.

Apology & forgiveness

"Love means never having to say your sorry," the theme from the movie "Love Story" has just one problem. One person died and the couple didn't get to see the long term damage of never having to say your sorry.

Key strategy: On a regular basis, practice the three A's of successful relationships: apologize for something from the past, appreciate something in the present, and anticipate something in the future.

Creating a relationship vision

Most couples spend more time planning a three day get away than they do planning what kind of marriage they would like to have. Vision has been defined as "the ability to see beyond the probable by envisioning the possible....... the act of dreaming without restriction opens up possibilities that you could not have considered before...."

Key strategy: Ask your self and each other this question: "If we knew we couldn't fail, and we could design our relationship any way that we wanted it, how would we like it to be?"

ACTION QUESTIONS

1) How would your relationship change if you used each of these 7 seeds?
2) Which one does your marriage need the most & right away?
3) Start planting!

Every effort has been made to attribute quotes to the proper source. If we have overlooked something, please let us know at: 1589 Metropolitan Blvd. Suite A Tallahassee, FL 32308.

Who is Jef Herring?

Jef Herring is a professional speaker, marriage & family counselor, clinical hypnotherapist, author, internationally syndicated columnist & success & change coach. He has spent the last 20 years helping people achieve the changes they want in their lives.

Jef's award winning weekly column originates in the Tallahassee Democrat and is run nationally and internationally through Knight-Ridder/Tribune Media Services. He is the author of several booklets, including: *Riding the Waves of Change: Becoming a Master of Change.*

Jef addresses hundreds of groups each year and is a regular guest on radio and TV. His clients include professional organizations, schools, churches, corporations, clubs and sales organizations.

Jef is the director of Jef Herring & Associates/ Strengthening the Family/Success & Change Technologies in Tallahassee, Fl. His award winning web-site, "Keep the Changes: Tools for Successful Living", can be found at **www.jeffherring.com.**

Jef believes "whether in speaking, writing or in private consultations, my job is simply to be a "change coach", to help people get the changes they want in their life: quickly, effectively, and lasting. And to have fun on the way."

To contact Jef for further information about his personal consultation/coaching sessions, books, posters, and tapes, or to schedule him for one of his dynamic presentations, please write or call:

Jef Herring
1589 Metropolitan Blvd Suite A Tallahassee, FL 32308
email:jherring@tdo.infi.net
Call **1-850-309-2170** or fax **850-422-2469.**

Jef's Stuff

BOOKS - $15 each, 2 for $25   Total #   Total

Keep the Changes!: 52 Tools for Successful Living & Solutions You Can Take Home

Jef's first book of columns. **Contains 52 of his best columns on:**
- **Stress-Success-Motivation-Change**
- **Marriage & Relationships**
- **Parenting-Families-Teens**

BOOKLETS - $6 each, 2 for $10   Total #   Total Amt

The 7 Seeds for Growing a Loving Relationship

I Deserve Combat Pay: *The Survival Guide for Parents of Teens*

The BRAAVO Approach to Life: *Seeds for a Jubilant Journey*

A Diamond is Simply a Lump of Coal that Handled Stress Very Well

Goal Settting & Goal Getting: *How to Create a Compelling Year & Life*

Riding the Waves of Change: *How to Master Change*

What to Do if the Holidays Turn Blue

Holiday Gifts of Lasting Value

Beating the Bozos Without Becoming One: *Difficult People at Work*

MINI-POSTERS - $2 each, any 6 for $10, packs of 10 for $15

         Total #   Total Amt

Universal Laws for *Couples*

Universal Laws for *Parents of Teens*

Universal Laws for *Success*

Universal Laws for *Motivation*

Universal Laws for *Managing Stress*

Universal Laws for *Goal Setting & Goal Getting*

Universal Laws for *Change*

Universal Laws for *Blending Families*

Universal Laws for *Singles*

Universal Laws for *Organization*

Universal Laws for *Managing Depression*

Universal Laws for *Mental Health*

Universal Laws for *Parents of Toddlers & Pre-Schoolers*

Universal Laws for *Teachers*

Universal Laws for *Students*

Universal Laws for *Divorce Recovery*

Universal Laws for *Managing Anger*
Universal Laws for *Self Esteem*   **Total Amt**

_____

Florida Residents include 7% sales tax   _____
shipping(included in price)   _____
TOTAL (check-payable to Jef Herring, cash, money order)   _____

ORDER FORM

Name:_____

Address:_____

City:_____ **St:**_____
Zip:_____ **Phone:**_____

Send to: Jef Herring
1589 Metropolitan Blvd Suite A Tallahassee, FL 32308
850-309-2170